1177

UNDAUNTED

CHARKES C. NESBITT

Copyright © 2015 Charkes C. Nesbitt

All rights reserved. No part of this publication may be reproduced, stored in a retrieval system, or transmitted, in any form or in any means – by electronic, mechanical, photocopying, recording or otherwise – without prior written permission.

ISBN-13: 978-1523610525
ISBN-10: 1523610522

CONTENTS

Preface 1
Chapter 1 Ya-Yow and Babalu 3
Chapter 2 Home Alone 9
Chapter 3 "HRS" 13
Chapter 4 The Good Times 17
Chapter 5 Edna's Place 19
Chapter 6 Going Back Home 25
Chapter 7 Replacing Ya-Yow 31
Chapter 8 Family "Out", Family "In" 37
Chapter 9 Jo & Co. 43
Chapter 10 54th Street 45
Chapter 11 "God Is Love" 51
Chapter 12 "Inner City" 63
Chapter 13 The "Scotts" 73
Chapter 14 G. Holmes Braddock 77
Chapter 15 Not What I Envisioned 87
Chapter 16 Babalu Without The Banana Boat ... 91
Chapter 17 Duke 95
Chapter 18 Doing Me 109
Chapter 19 Moving On 115
Appendix 119

PREFACE

I began this journey about eight years ago. It was then when I became conscious of the things that were not going so well in my life. I was dating Corey, who claimed to have been in love with me for years before he actually did something about it. And despite the fact he was married, we began a whirlwind love affair. For the hundredth time, I found myself in an intimate relationship I had no business being in. The events of my relationship with Corey awakened something in me. I began to question who I was and I didn't like what I'd discovered. The depression I thought had gone away after I left my son's father was now back with a vengeance. I started documenting my feelings on paper, which in turn led to thoughts about my life in its entirety. Reflections of my mother would often cross my forebrain; I was beginning to see myself in her. From this, *1177* was conceived.

What I present to you is a journal of my journey. As I image my life, I hope that the lens you use to read this book will be an introverted one, offering reflection, conviction, and change. Finally, I hope my journey causes *you* to understand and accept *yourself.* Much peace and many blessings.

CHAPTER

YA-YOW AND BABALU

My name is Charkes Chaketha Nesbitt. I was born, January 1, 1977, at 8:32 a.m. at Jackson Memorial Hospital in Miami, Florida. I am my mother's third eldest child and the eighth of my father's eighteen children. My mother's name was Yolanda Yvette Buford. Her family affectionately called her "Yo-Yo." Our version was "Ya-Yow"—and this was how we referred to her until the day she died. Ya-Yow was beautiful. I remember her being about 5' 10" tall, slim though still curvy, and having a smile that would light up the world. Prior to giving birth to me, she had two sons who were each fathered by a different man.

My mother and father's union began in a local Miami nightclub. My father's band was one of its regular acts, and Ya-Yow was out that evening, dancing the night away. While performing, my father noticed Ya-Yow eyeing him. Once his first set was over, they went outside the club to talk and the rest is history.

My daddy's name is Edison Paul Nesbitt, better known as "Babalu." According to Babalu, the name came from a musical mentor of his who also went by the same moniker. Babalu was the founder, lead singer, and percussionist of Babalu and His Headhunters, a calypso band birthed in Nassau, Bahamas. By the time he and Ya-Yow met, the band was housed in his nightclub, Babalu's Banana Boat, or just the Banana Boat. The club was located on 49th Street and 7th Avenue. Babalu opened it after falling out with the owners of the Elks Lodge, a club across the street from the Banana Boat. Babalu spent most of his time there. If he wasn't singing, he was cooking. He wasn't a formal chef but could cook like no other. He would fry fish, which was always seasoned to perfection, and make chicken souse and conch salad that was sold to the bar patrons. And although we were only allowed to share a cup of conch salad between every two of us, we were responsible for dicing every vegetable that the recipe called for.

Babalu often had us work in the Banana Boat, mainly Keo and me. He would pick us up on Saturday mornings to sweep and mop the entire club. I still remember the stench of stale beer and cigarettes that would hit my nostrils as soon as I'd walk in. Believe it or not, there was a sense of excitement associated with those trips to the Banana Boat. This would be especially heightened when I found a dollar or two while cleaning. Keo and I would also have to accompany Babalu to the liquor and beer warehouse. We would sit in the car while he made his purchases and help him unload once we returned to the club. We were given strict instructions on how to stock the coolers. Bottles and cans of Becks, Heineken, Miller, Budweiser,

Ya-Yow and Babalu

and Guinness beer were stacked neatly, one after the other until they reached the top. We would also have to stack nonalcoholic beverages that included coconut-flavored Yoo-hoos, our favorite. I'd trade anything to have a bottle all to myself. Keo would often serve as the bartender during the day and a semi-DJ at night, making sure the jukebox was on constant rotation in between sets. This went on for years. I honestly don't understand how Babalu didn't get in trouble for all of the crimes he committed by having Keo and me behind the bar. Especially given that one of his friends and customers was a City of Miami police officer.

Babalu had a record deal with Bamboo Records, which produced Bahamian hits like "Mr. Pindling," "Calypso Funk," and "The Bahamas Gone Independent." You could hear him belting these hits along with the American songs he usually covered ("Say You, Say Me" by Lionel Ritchie, for instance) on the weekends at the Banana Boat. I would often make up reasons to go to the club just so that I could hear him perform. I could hear my daddy before I could see him. The club would be so packed with patrons that I would have to bend and curl in order to get to the bandstand. As I excused myself through the crowd, I could overhear people saying, "That's Babalu's oldest daughter. Boy she pretty, aye," in heavily Bahamian-accented voices. I'd finally reach the bandstand but then would have to wait until Babalu finished his set. With his microphone settled to the left of him, eyes closed and drumsticks in hand, he would sing, "Don't squeeze the mango, don't squeeze the mango, all of them are sweet you know, so don't squeeze the mango." The people would wind and twirl to the lyrics as if they didn't have a care in the world. I didn't know it at the time, but my love for live music had begun.

Babalu's lifestyle precluded a functional relationship with Ya-Yow. He spent most of his time at the club, which more than displeased her. My guess is that she was disappointed because she thought he would slow down or that things would change once they got together. Despite his unavailability, she continued to have children from him. Ten months after I was born, Ya-Yow had a son. And from 1979 to 1984, she had a baby every year.

My first and worst memory of my mother was the first time she left me home alone. We were living in an apartment complex near Jackson Memorial Hospital. As she walked from her bedroom to the front door, I threw a tantrum that I can still remember to this day. I kicked, screamed, and cried. Where was she going? I couldn't imagine there being any place more important than at home with me, her baby girl. I soon found out Ya-Yow was leaving me at home in order to keep up with my dad. This became a common practice that she obviously had no conscience about. I had no idea at the time how that moment would impact my life. I would forever be in search of that woman who left me in the middle of the floor more than thirty years ago.

Babalu was unavailable to Ya-Yow, and she was even more unavailable to us. The only time I would see my father was when he came home for sex with Ya-Yow or to drop off portions of food. He came home for the former more often than the latter. I would see Ya-Yow getting ready for his arrival. She would don a half-black slip, pulling it up to cover her breasts, wearing nothing underneath. My mother was as shapely as I am now, so the slip would accentuate her hips, making it look like a sexy minidress. The bed linen would be changed. Because our rooms were side by side, separated by a window, I could hear my mother moaning as my daddy made love to her. I could hear her enjoying the only moment she could have Babalu all to herself. I'd take a peak from time to time, curious about what they were doing. Upon waking the next morning, I'd walk into their room, pretending to need something, and always see a bunched up washcloth sitting on the nightstand. It was the washcloth Ya-Yow had used repeatedly to clean the leftover cum from Babalu's penis.

Because Babalu spent most of his conscious time at the Banana Boat he was afforded a plethora of opportunities to meet and date other women. This became obvious to Ya-Yow and she made it her business to go to the Banana Boat to mark her territory. Just about every weekend, Ya-Yow and the youngest child would go to the club (leaving me to look after everyone else), and sit at the bar for hours, just so she could keep up with Babalu, and more so, make it difficult for him to carry out a relationship with another woman. I could only imagine what Babalu would say when he saw her walking into the club with her booty shorts on and a baby in tow.

Despite Ya-Yow's efforts, Babalu managed to

1177: Undaunted

forge a romantic relationship with another woman. Physically, she was the opposite of Ya-Yow. Her skin was darker, ass extraordinarily bigger, and she fell short of Ya-Yow about 2-3 inches. She and her five children lived in a nearby housing project. And like Ya-Yow, she would leave her babies home alone so that she could spend time with her man. Eventually, she became Babalu's part-time bartender, or "barmaid" as my dad would say. She and Ya-Yow were well aware of each other and their place in Babalu's life. They had a sort of antagonistic yet peaceful relationship—hating each other while getting along for fear of losing my daddy.

As life would have it, she began to experience the same torment Ya-Yow did—the pain of being the other woman. The seemingly perfect relationship (to her) inevitably revealed itself as the ball of toxicity it always was. She and Babalu fought like cats and dogs. She'd make her way to the Banana Boat by cab and tear up everything in sight. Babalu had an office in the back where he slept and cooked food. I recall numerous occasions where I'd walk back there and see the remnants of her hurricane. But they stayed together—all three of them.

Chapter

Home Alone

All sorts of things would happen when we were left alone, and that includes my first injury. I was standing in the empty part of our duplex that led to the living room. There was a glass door that separated the two areas. Frustrated because my younger brothers, Keo and Duke, weren't listening to me, I kicked the door, severing my right calf. I was hysterical. Blood was everywhere and there wasn't an adult in sight. We didn't have a phone so I couldn't call anyone either. I think I passed out because the next thing I remembered was Ya-Yow rushing me to Jackson Hospital. While we sat in the emergency room waiting to be seen, I went to the bathroom to pee. For some reason, I felt really tired so I lay on the bathroom floor and eventually fell asleep. I could only imagine what onlookers thought, seeing a little girl lying on a public bathroom floor. Come to think about it, they may have thought I was dead. Ya-Yow eventually came to get me. She had an annoyed look on her face, likely because of all of the trouble I was causing her. I ended up with multiple stitches that day. My scar is a constant reminder of that duplex.

And then there was Simone's injury. For some

1177: Undaunted

reason, Simone thought straddling the kitchen cabinet and swinging from side to side would be fun. I'd repeatedly told her to get off the cabinet before she hurt herself, and in good ole "Simone fashion" she didn't. The next thing I heard was her screaming my name, "Charkes!" I ran to the kitchen and there she was: standing in the middle of the floor with blood sliding down her left thigh. I was frantic. Ya-Yow was going to kill me when she got home; because I wasn't watching the kids like I should have been, one of her babies had gotten hurt. I immediately stripped her naked and threw her in the tub. I don't know what I thought that would do, but it was the first thing that came to mind. As I looked for the source of the bleeding, the blood began to mix with the water to the point that there appeared to be more blood than water. Simone then became frantic. I pulled her out of the tub, laid her on the bed, and opened her legs, all the while continuing to search for the source. Finally I found it. There was a cut to the left side of her outer coochie lip and it was still bleeding. While swinging on the cabinet, she must have lost her balance, causing the edge of the cabinet to impale her skin. All while trying to keep Simone calm, I grabbed a towel and pressed down as hard as I could. The bleeding eventually stopped. Talk about a close call. Had Ya-Yow come home to see what had happened, my ass would have been in a world of trouble. I think both Simone and I ended up taking naps after that. I didn't know about her but I was exhausted from playing emergency personnel and from constantly thinking about Ya-Yow during the emergency.

Home Alone

A couple of our (older) first cousins lived next door to us. They were brothers and my father's oldest sister's sons. One was pretty low key so I don't remember much about him. The other was the exact opposite. He wasn't loud but when he was around you could feel his presence. He stood about 6' tall and was stout. Although relatively unimportant, he would always park his company truck in the yard. It was always annoying because the truck was huge, requiring him to occupy both yard spaces. Babalu would always curse him out, telling him to "get his fucking truck out of his yard." From time to time, a young boy—who I thought was their brother but it turned out was one of their sons—would visit from the Bahamas. And because we were close in age, he'd come and hang out with us. One day he came over and asked me to go into my parents' bedroom. Although an odd request, I carried it out. He then asked that I lie on the bed, after which he pulled my bottoms down. The next thing I remember was him inserting his little penis into my coochie. There was no thrusting or moving back and forth, he just stuck it in. I knew what he was doing because I had watched my parents do it all of the time. And like me, he had likely witnessed adults carelessly having sex around him. This was the first of many instances of sexual molestation I would experience.

Ya-Yow would punish me when things went wrong while she was gone. No matter if I was directly to blame, she made it clear that when she left me in charge I was to make sure everything remained in order. Punishment would involve verbal

11

and physical abuse. She would use belts, switches, boards, and even the rubber lining used to hold the screen in its frame. I remember a time when she beat me fresh out of the bathtub. I was not allowed to dry off, so you could imagine the pain I felt every time the belt hit my skin. I was a little bitty thing too. I had all sorts of welts on my body. I would cry uncontrollably, not only because of the physical hurt but because of the emotional pain as well. I was confused. I tried my best to do exactly what Ya-Yow asked me to do, but it never seemed to be good enough. Although I didn't comprehend it then, I eventually came to understand that she was beating me out of frustration. It wasn't me she was mad at. She was mad at herself for being in love with a man who gave less than a damn about her or the children she bore for him. She was also mad at *her* mother for treating her horribly, leading her to such a man. Ya-Yow was projecting her emotions onto me. As I close my eyes, I'm taken back to the expressions on her face and the anger, hate, and sadness behind every hit.

Chapter

"HRS"

The Banana Boat was Babalu's home. His friends were there, his band was there, and his women were there, even Ya-Yow, on the weekends. And as I mentioned earlier, he would come home for sex and to bring us portions of food from time to time. On Saturday mornings, his brown station wagon would pull up on the sidewalk. Most of the time his good friend Rubber Duck would accompany him. Both of them would always appear tired from the night before. To make his arrival known, Babalu would blow his horn and either Ya-Yow or I would go outside to fetch whatever he had brought. I remember him bringing a dozen Krispy Kreme doughnuts home once. Grateful for whatever we could get, we ate those doughnuts slowly and carefully, savoring their deliciousness while not wanting to drop a morsel. After all, we didn't know where our next meal would come from. In addition, you never wanted to be the first one finished, having to watch everyone else eat his or hers, charming you. Although I have grown to understand a great deal of what my parents experienced individually and as a couple, there is one thing that continues to baffle me. At least one of them should have felt like it was appropriate to provide us with at least one full meal per day. They both were so consumed with themselves and their relationships that they neglected the products of their relationship.

As time went on, our neighbors became aware of what was going on and they did something about it. I remember the first day I met them. There was a knock at the door, and despite strict instructions from Ya-Yow, I opened the door to see who was there. I saw a white man and woman staring into my face and asking, "Is your mother or father home?" By then, I had grown tired of my parents' shenanigans. I expeditiously replied, "No." And in a simultaneous manner, they asked to come in and walked through our front door. With every step through our duplex, there was notation of the extent of neglect we were experiencing. They finally made it to the kitchen, the area that would dot all i's and cross all t's. The woman entered before the man and went straight to the refrigerator. I stood to the side as an innocent bystander. The fridge's contents revealed the greatest degree of neglect one could imagine. The only things in the refrigerator were a jug of water, mayonnaise, and a bread loaf bag that contained two end pieces. From the looks on the caseworkers' faces, they had seen enough. The next thing I remember was my siblings and I being carried away in a police car.

That visit landed us in a group home. My guess is that a group home was the only place that could accommodate so many children on such short notice. We arrived in the wee hours of the morning, and although my memory falls short in regard to how long we were there, I can recall my experience there with great detail. I was allowed to survey the house, and while doing so, I came across a little boy in a crib. His face and body habitus proved he was not an infant. However, his mental state matched the bed he was lying in. I was like a deer caught in headlights, staring at him. His limbs were contracted and he moaned continuously. I imagine he had been born with those anomalies and his parents had been unable to bear the burden of caring for him. Finally, I got into bed to retire for the night. I don't know if anyone was in the room with me, but that didn't matter because no level of company could take away the emotion I was feeling. My surroundings were unfamiliar and I was afraid. I felt extremely lonely and wanted my mom more than ever. In the background I could hear the ceaseless moans of the little boy I'd encountered earlier. He likely felt as afraid and sad as I did.

CHAPTER

THE GOOD TIMES

Despite such grave circumstances, I have some good memories of my early childhood. I would wake up early on Saturday mornings to catch "America's Top 10," a syndicated music show hosted by Casey Kasem that aired the top ten songs of the past week and included the pop, R&B, and country genres. Sitting in an Indian-style position for thirty minutes, I'd watch and listen to music legends like Pat Benatar, Cyndi Lauper, Rick Springfield, and Michael Jackson. I can still hear and feel the beat of the introduction to "Love is a Battlefield." "We are young, heartache to heartache, we stand." But my all-time favorite was Michael Jackson and Paul McCartney's "Say, Say, Say." The video brought R&B, pop, and country music into a beautiful combination highlighted by its vaudeville-themed video. These musicians, along with my daddy, helped to form my feelings and beliefs about music. This show centered me and took me away from my reality, even for only thirty minutes a week.

On occasion, Ya-Yow would come out of her Babalu-related funk and fall into her role as a mother. I remember mornings when she'd take extra care in getting me ready for school, putting my hair in two poof ponytails—like the ones in the picture on the cover of this book. I was happiest during our walks to and from school. She would always hold my hand really tight, making sure I didn't run into the streets. I would feel protected.

I was only four years old when I started school. My fifth birthday fell during the January after the school year began, so the middle of the school year. Unless I wanted to wait until the next school year to enroll, I would have to take an entrance exam. So, I did. We lived close to the school, so it only took us ten or so minutes to get there. I sat down at a long table in what I remember was the school's cafeteria. Before me were multiple flashcards containing shapes, words, and numbers. The shapes were brainteasers. I had to really think about what was being implied and not simply state what I saw. Needless to say, I passed the test and was able attend kindergarten at Arcola Lakes Elementary at four years old.

Ya-Yow would surprise me with gifts. She would interrupt my class (showing up in her shortest shorts) to bring me batons—the ones that band majorettes used. Yeah, I would feel extra special during those times. Who would ever figure that I would end up being a part of a marching band in college, not as a majorette, but as a dancer?

Chapter

Edna's Place

After countless times of being left alone, my siblings and I were eventually placed into foster care. And because there were so many of us, we had to be separated. India and I were sent to live in Naranja, Florida, with Edna, while Simone was around the corner with Edna's sister, Catherine. Edna was a beyond middle-aged African-American woman who was married to Anthony, a garbage truck worker. Edna was the mother of three children: Audrey, Michael, and Angela. Michael and Angela, along with Edna's grandson Fats, lived at home, and Audrey lived in a neighboring city. Edna worked for Good Will, collecting donations. She was the person settled at the back of the Good Will trucks you'd see in vacant parking lots. To me, she had the greatest job. She would bring home baby dolls, skates, and games. We even got our first bicycles from the Good Will truck. I was in heaven. For the first time in my life, I was allowed uninterrupted child time. I could be my age and my age only—no looking after children, being in charge, or worrying about child protective services coming to the door. It was the best.

1177: Undaunted

Edna and Anthony had a huge five-bedroom house that included a family room, a formal living room, and a dining room. India and I shared a room. We had bunk beds, a matching dresser and mirror, and our very own color television. The best part of the house was the huge backyard that extended to each side of the house. There was a huge oak tree that I loved to play in. It held a tire swing on one of its larger branches. I'd sit on the tire while my neighbor turned it until its rope reached its tightest. And once it did, he'd let it go, watching me unwind with the rope. That was so much fun. Well, at least until I fell off the tire and hit my head on the tree stump. Physically, I was okay, but my feelings were hurt. I was done with that damn tire and tree. My ass never touched that rubber again.

I don't remember too much about Audrey, except that she was beautiful. She stood about as tall as I am now, and her skin was a smooth coffee color after you added creamer. Her hair was long, jet black, and settled in the middle of her back. She would come around from time to time. Otherwise, she stayed below the radar and attended to her family. She had boys close to my age, so I hung out at her house on occasion. It was there where I first played an Atari game—Galaga, to be exact. Galaga was a single-player game (as most were back then) where you had control of a spacecraft positioned at the bottom of the screen. Using the spacecraft, you had to kill oncoming aliens before the two collided.

Michael was the most fun. He had to be in his early 20s and was a Prince fanatic. "Purple Rain" had just come out and he couldn't get enough of the movie or the album. He also liked Michael Jackson like I did, so he was definitely cool with me.

Fats was in his late teens. He was tall, had a medium build, and always serious. Fats was also Audrey's eldest son. She was young so I imagine she must have had him when she was just a teenager herself. Fats had a lot of legal troubles that caused him to live with Edna and Anthony. Audrey couldn't handle him and he definitely didn't fit in with the "white picket fence life" she had at the time. I was afraid of Fats. Not only because of his unsmiling face, but because he violated me. At times, he was our babysitter when Edna and Anthony went out. He'd demand that I sleep in his room, which was located at the front of the house. Once everyone was asleep (except for me), he'd stand in the doorframe, staring at me as I lay in bed. His presence was palpable, even before he laid a hand on me. As he walked over, I'd tighten my eyes and body, preparing myself for what was to come. And all at once, my covers were down, my nightgown up, and his hands were in my panties fondling my coochie. Surprisingly, he never attempted to penetrate me. There were times when Edna would come home and find me in Fats's bed. She never questioned it, though. I imagine the idea of Fats molesting me never crossed Edna's mind.

And lastly, there was Edna's youngest child and daughter, Angela. Affectionately called "Angie," she was a senior in high school, which made her about seventeen or eighteen years old. Angie wasn't very tall but she was built like a grown woman. This likely attracted all of the men she dated. Grown men would pick her up in fancy cars and take her

1177: Undaunted

wherever she wanted to go. As time went on, I would tag along. We mainly went to the mall and to the movies. My relationship with Angie was awesome; she was like the big sister I never had. The closer we got, the more I wanted to be around her. And although I loved the room India and I shared, Angie's room became my own. At night, I would lie on one side of her, gazing at the ceiling and thinking about how life was so much better for me. And then something happened. Naturally, I'd go to bed before Angie but I would usually wait until she got into bed before I fell asleep. One particular night, I noticed her putting her hand into her panties. Because I had been exposed to sex at such an early age, I knew exactly what she was doing. I quietly and subtly watched as she rubbed her coochie in search of that one spot that would cause her to climax. I'm more than positive she knew I was watching, meaning she was comfortable with including me in her sessions. She then took my hand, slid it down to her clit, and moved it around and around, up and down until my fingers were exactly where she wanted them to be. As she controlled my hand, I lay as still as I could, staring at the tightening of her eyes and lips, signs that she was pleased. The encounters with Angie and Fats went on for as long as I can remember. And until I became an adult, I never told a soul. I knew doing so would put me at risk of losing the life I had come to love. I also knew that Angie would get in trouble and I wasn't going to do that to her—I loved her too much.

I have had a great number of heterosexual

relationships, too many to count. I often wonder if being exposed to and involved in sex at such an early age contributed to my promiscuity. I mean, the psychology surrounding sexual encounters with key people in your life—people who are supposed to guide and protect you—has to condition you to believe that sex is the primary way love is conveyed. Ya-Yow and Babalu were only happy when they had sex. My older cousin molested me, and then Fats and Angie did the same thing. An expert can provide a more layered insight but it likely will not be much different from my explanation.

Chapter

Going Back Home

My teacher beckoned me to her office, saying someone wanted to see me. It was a Human Resource Services (HRS) social worker. As I sat across from her, I was filled with anxiety, knowing all too well what she was there for. She went on to tell me that my older siblings had gone to visit my parents and I was going to accompany the younger ones on the next visit. My mouth agreed but my mind and heart were saying no. And before I knew it, I was headed to my parents' house. By this time they were settled in a duplex on 14th Avenue and 60th Street (1456 N.W. 60th Street). There were two bedrooms, one bathroom, a living space, and a kitchen. One of the bedrooms was designated for us. It contained two sets of bunk beds, two children per bunk. Everyone seemed to be on their best behavior. There was food, and plenty of parental supervision. We saw Ya-Yow and Babalu the entire weekend—a rarity. When I got back to my foster parents' home, the social worker probed me to see how the visit had gone. My response was a mere "okay." She continued to ask more detailed questions about Babalu and Ya-Yow and I replied as

1177: Undaunted

honestly as I could. I mean, they were my parents, and naturally, I loved them, but I didn't want to live with them. I wanted to be with Edna, Anthony, and Angie—the people I saw as my real family. And just like my gut told me, the visit was a set up to send us back to my parents for good.

Late in the school day, the social worker picked me up, put me in the back of her car, and told me that I was going home. I didn't even get a chance to tell Edna and Anthony good-bye. They were still at work. We stopped by the house to get India and to gather some of my belongings, and as we walked out of the door, I could hear Michael say, "Momma is gonna be mad as hell when she comes home and finds out her children are gone. " I looked back but continued to walk forward. The minute I got into the back of the car, the tears started to fall. I don't know if you remember the scene from the movie *Losing Isaiah*? I liken that little boy's emotion to mine. And although he was going back to his biological mother, he knew he was being taken away from the people who truly loved him—the people who understood him. I cried myself to sleep.

We'd finally arrived. Tired from crying and my heart's heaviness, the only thing I wanted to do was lie down. Before I walked through the doors of what was my new home, the social worker stopped me. She handed me a contact card that contained her full name and phone number. She directed me to call if I needed anything. I wanted to tell her right then and there that I wanted to go back home. I wanted to go back to Naranja to live with Edna and Anthony. Knowing that wasn't an option, I lightly nodded "okay" and walked into the house. I wouldn't say a full week had passed before I was trying to call the social worker. The minute I felt like I was being mistreated, I dialed those seven numbers. Early on, the social worker would talk me through the situations, but my phone calls soon fell on deaf ears. She stopped answering and returning my calls. I was on my own.

Despite almost losing us, Babalu maintained his position. He kept the Banana Boat up and running and went back to spending most of his time there. But Ya-Yow stayed put. No longer was she leaving me at home, gallivanting in the street, trying to keep up with Babalu. She was home with us, all day, every day. I wonder if she remained at home at her own will? Did she finally care more about us than about him and their toxic relationship? Or was she forced to stay home by Babalu? Around this time Ya-Yow started acting differently. She began having conversations with herself. I'd see her talking, crying, and cursing while focused on a corner wall in our living room, where she usually slept. The conversations were volatile, like those in toxic romantic relationships. She'd respond when spoken to but given the hallucinations she was experiencing, it was hard to determine if her answers were given in lucidity. The many years of abuse and neglect appeared to be manifesting themselves in ways I, as a child, couldn't begin to understand. I, like everyone else, thought my mom had gone "crazy."

In addition to the hallucinatory conversations,

1177: Undaunted

Ya-Yow began wearing layers of clothes. Despite the scorching Miami heat, she'd don two to three shirts, including a long-sleeved one, a long pair of pants, and a pair of shorts. She would also collect soda can tops. Wherever she found them, she'd pick them up and, one at a time, put them on whatever piece of string she had, making a necklace. She'd also collect rings or anything that resembled one. This became one of her favorite pastimes. All ten of her fingers would usually be adorned in her self-made jewelry.

Despite all of this, Ya-Yow and Babalu continued to be physically intimate. The night of October 27, 1987, proved it. While lying in bed in the dark (Babalu failed to pay the electric bill), I heard Ya-Yow call my name. The urgency in her voice caused me to jump up as quickly as I could to see what she wanted. Before I could bend the corner that separated our room from the living room, which by then was her primary living quarters, she shouted, "Go next door and call the ambulance!" Without a second thought I ran outside to our neighbors' house. I don't remember who answered the door, but they knew what I was there for. Upon returning home, I could hear a baby crying. I couldn't believe it. Who even knew she was pregnant? And even more astounding was the fact that she delivered the damn baby herself. Holy shit, I thought. No more than five minutes later the ambulance had arrived. The cries of a newborn immediately made them aware of why they'd been summoned to our house. I overheard one of the medical personnel ask Ya-Yow if she had delivered the baby herself. Quietly, she responded, "Yes." With my new baby sister wrapped in her arms, Ya-Yow was transported to Jackson Memorial

Hospital. She named her Shadeaw (Shadow) because she had been born in the dark.

I assume that Babalu had sense enough to know Ya-Yow was not in a position to care for another child, let alone a newborn. I wouldn't have been able to do it either. Shadeaw was eventually sent to live with Babalu's eldest sister in the Bahamas. We wouldn't see her again for at least three years.

CHAPTER 7

REPLACING YA-YOW

Ya-Yow's condition worsened. She became more and more irate in her conversations and began to neglect her personal hygiene. She wasn't bathing or brushing her teeth. The only thing she actually attended to was her hair. She'd stopped cutting it and finally ended up with a curly afro. She would part it down the middle and across her head and then give herself four huge dukie plaits. She also started going to the Banana Boat again. This would have been okay if she hadn't insisted that we go with her. On any given day, she would gather all eight of us and walk (what was then six or seven miles) to the Banana Boat. She'd even come to the school to pick us up. We were all attending Orchard Villa Elementary by then. My and Keo's classes were on the second floor, where there was a window that gave us a view of the corner Ya-Yow had to turn to get to the school. Once I spotted her (with the younger kids in tow) I'd alert Keo and we would break off running, not wanting to take that long ass walk to the bar. She'd see us running and call our names, directing us to bring our asses to her. I suspect someone noticed what was going on with

1177: Undaunted

Ya-Yow because before I knew it, she was gone. Ya-Yow was labeled "unfit" and therefore could not live with us anymore. I honestly don't know where she went. Babalu never uttered another word about her.

Ya-Yow was now gone, so naturally I had to take on her responsibilities. At ten years old, I had to cook, clean, wash clothes, and do hair. The cooking and cleaning were okay, but what I hated most was going to the damn washhouse, mainly because we went in the wee hours of the morning. This time was more suitable for Babalu because he would be done at the Banana Boat by then. Babalu would come home and awaken me, saying, "Charkes, get up an let's go to the washhouse." I would dump all of our clothes in the middle of a sheet and secure them by folding the sheet's corners in fours. Whatever couldn't fit in the sheet would be stuffed into pillowcases. We'd always go to the washhouse across the street from the Banana Boat (To date, that washhouse is still in business.) Once we got there, Babalu would take the clothes out for me, sit them in front of a "Big Boy" washer, and hand me twenty-five dollars to wash clothes for eight kids. Oh, and I almost forgot to mention: I would also have to fit washing powder and bleach into that budget. Needless to say, all of the colors went into one washer and the whites in another. While I was working hard, Babalu would be reclined in the front seat of his car with his damn mouth wide open, sleeping. And after about two and a half hours, I was done. I never folded the clothes. I just dumped them all back into their makeshift containers so that I could get home and get a little

Replacing Ya-Yow

rest before school. If I had change, I'd keep it to buy myself a honey bun as a reward for being so responsible.

While home alone, we'd get into all sorts of things. One particular day, three of my siblings were pouring alcohol on their hands and setting them a fire. Once lit, they'd shake their hands vigorously from side to side until the fire was extinguished. I thought it was pretty cool, so I tried it. I extended my right hand and Keo poured alcohol on its dorsal portion. Once lit, I shook it from side to side like I'd seen everyone else do. But guess what, my goddamn hand remained on fire. I shook and shook and shook but nothing happened. I finally got enough sense to get up and run to the kitchen where I submerged my hand in water. The fire was out but my hand continued to feel the burn. I was in an extreme amount of pain and didn't know what to do. Following the old adage about butter soothing burns, I went into the refrigerator, grabbed the tiny piece that was sitting in the door, and slathered it all over my hand. And guess what, my damn hand was still on fire. Shortly after, everyone walked into the house with frozen cups they'd just bought from the candy lady's house. I'd found my cure. After I demanded that everyone give me their frozen cup, I dumped them into a basin Babalu had used after his abdominal surgery and positioned my hand underneath the juice-filled ice blocks. I did feel temporary relief, but anyone that knows anything about burns knows that I felt pain for another two weeks (at least).

1177: Undaunted

Hunger was commonplace for us. We felt the pain often. Just as when we were younger, Babalu would buy food occasionally, leaving us to walk the streets looking for soda bottles that we could sell for fifteen cents apiece. Collecting about ten would get us a soda, chips, a honey bun, and maybe a couple packs of Jingles. Jingles were candies similar to Now and Laters, but smaller. I remember a time when my school, Orchard Villa, held a fund-raiser. You know the ones that require students to sell candy? Back then, they'd give us the candy to sell and we were expected to return the monies by a given deadline. I'd sell the candy and keep the money so that I could buy food. Every time my teacher would ask about it, I'd lie and say I hadn't completed my sales. Eventually, she figured out what was going on. I was using the school's fund-raiser as a "Charkes Family fund-raiser."

On one of our many hungry days, a few of us were looking out of our bedroom window and witnessed our neighbor scraping leftovers into his trash can. Our heads moved synchronously with each raking movement, we watched him throw away fried fish and rice. By the last stroke, we had all concluded that our neighbor's trash would soon be our treasure. Immediately, we ran outside and picked out every piece of fish that was salvageable. We stood and ate directly from the trash can. Within minutes of going back into the house, his wife delivered a huge serving of sausage and rice to our door, along with two City of Miami Police officers. My younger siblings recall my brother Keo and I jumping out of our parents' bedroom window and hauling ass to God knows where while the rest of them were barraged with questions about our parents' whereabouts and whether or not they had eaten. Eventually, they were put in the back of the police car, taken to the station where they were fed, and then brought back home. One would think that incident would have won us a trip to a foster home, but just like our social worker, the police looked the other way.

Chapter

Family "Out", Family "In"

Our lives were nothing short of surprises and turns of events. Like most families, we had members who were hard on their luck and needed a place to lay their heads. This was something I looked forward to because it provided a sense of stability. Always an adult, the family member would usually cook, clean, and more important, look after us. I especially enjoyed them being there because I was provided relief from my own adult responsibilities. My favorite was our cousin Dion. Affectionately nicknamed "Buzzard," Dion came to live with us after he and his wife had separated. I also remember him lightly mentioning their only child dying of "crib death." We know this now as Sudden Infant Death Syndrome (SIDS). Dion stood about 5' 11", had a full beard, mustache, and a lean, muscular frame. Most notable was the gap between his two front teeth. Like Michael Strahan, it was hard to imagine his teeth being any other way. They were perfectly imperfect. His temperament was mild most times but I sensed that there was another side of him that was the exact opposite. I liked Dion a lot. Not only because of the relief he provided but also because he was a naturally caring person. He was genuinely concerned about our wellbeing and was always empathetic to the burden I bared in caring for my siblings.

I honestly can't remember how long Dion lived with us, but I do remember an incident that may have led to his departure. As Dion stood on the sidewalk in front of our duplex, a car rolled up alongside of him. On our porch was another man who I was more than familiar with because he had made our porch his "drug hole." The driver of the car yelled, "Hey, you, come here." Of course, Dion thought he was talking to him so he responded. Pointing at the man on our porch, the driver replied, "Not you, him." And before I could blink, the driver pulled out a gun and started shooting. Immediately, I closed the door and dropped to the floor. After hearing the car speed away, I gathered myself and looked out of our front room window to see if Dion was okay. As I pulled back the bedroom sheet that covered the window, I saw the other man lying supine in a pool of blood. I quickly moved my eyes outward to reassess the scene, and after seeing the coast was clear, I opened the door. His eyes were closed and he was shivering uncontrollably while whispering, "I'm cold." I had no idea what to do and neither did the slew of people that had suddenly gathered around him. I stood in the doorway, frozen like a deer trapped in headlights. The ambulance eventually made its way to the man. For days afterward, Dion and I replayed that situation, moment after moment, verbally and nonverbally.

We continued to encounter similar violence in

Family "Out", Family "In"

that neighborhood. Our neighbor's daughter was killed while at a nearby birthday party. We eventually moved.

Our next stop was between 15th and 17th Avenues on 69th Street. Babalu had managed to find us a nice-sized three-bedroom, one-bathroom house with a den. An elderly woman lived to our left, whom I only saw when she was leaving for church. And to our right was a middle-aged couple whose daughter and grandson lived with them. Although things weren't as violent as they were on 60th Street, the noise of prostitution and drug dealing that encased us resonated as loudly as the gunshots I'd seen and heard at our previous residence. Most times we remained indoors, fearful of what Babalu would do if he found us outside. When we did go out we were okay because we had learned Babalu's patterns; we could predict his arrival. There was one instance that told our secret, though. My younger brother Chaz was running in our yard, playing with a dog we'd found on the street and adopted (informally). Around and around in circles, Chaz and the dog chased each other. And although he was having fun, I sat on the porch worried—worried that Chaz might fall. It rained that day, so the yard was wet and slippery. My fearful thoughts became a reality. Chaz slipped and fell on a tree stump, landing on his right arm. And guess what? His goddamn arm was broken. I don't know who took us, but both Chaz and I ended up in Jackson Memorial Hospital's emergency room. Our ages—11 and 6—prevented us from getting treatment until one of our parents was able to provide consent. There were no cell phones back then, nor did we have a house phone, so we sat in the emergency room for hours before Babalu appeared. And when he finally showed up, he nonchalantly told us he had been out on a boat performing. I assume he'd gone home and one of the other siblings told him what had happened.

As I write, I am amazed at the number of times we encountered the police or individuals that could report our situation to social services but never did. I mean, even though he got a pass on the trash can incident, you would think that having your minor child sit in an emergency room for hours, with a fractured arm no less, would at least land him in some sort of child rearing–improvement program. Someone or something bigger was obviously in control of our lives.

The second person from my dad's family to temporarily live with us was his sister Dora. She came to help out my dad at the Banana Boat. He and his side chick were done by then so Dora would serve as his barmaid. Dora was short with long hair. She had skin that was dark and smooth like chocolate. What I remember most about my aunt were her drunken conversations. She was a heavy drinker, unable to draw the line between feeling nice and getting wasted. I imagine working at the Banana Boat made that line close to invisible. If she hadn't totally passed out in a drunken stupor, she'd come home and tell me all about Smokey, her boyfriend at the time. And in her sleep, she would

Family "Out", Family "In"

call his name, repeatedly, as if she were mourning him. But as quickly as Dora came, she went back home to Nassau. She and Smokey eventually had a little girl but their relationship dissolved.

Then there was my dad's cousin, Mae. Like Dion, I liked Mae, a lot. Mae was intelligent and spoke perfect English—I always admired her excellent diction and extensive vocabulary. Mae loved to read. One might even consider her love for literature an addiction. I think she could put away a 500-pager in a couple of days. But Mae had another addiction: narcotics. I was confused by the juxtaposition of her love for literature and her addiction to narcotics. Throughout my childhood, I was constantly exposed to people who were addicted to drugs. They looked a certain way, were products of poverty, and always uneducated—at least from my visual field. But not Mae. She was never disheveled or the frame of skin and bones I had grown accustomed to seeing. Her mother was a businesswoman who was more than capable of taking care of herself, Mae, and her children. And the knowledge attained from reading made her far from uneducated, despite not attending college.

On a regular basis, I'd see Mae walking down 69th Street from 17th Avenue. She'd always appear exhausted. I assume our house was her rest stop. As soon as she got into the house, she'd take a shower and finish settling by curling up with a book. Mae would usually stay with us for a day or two, after which she would hit the streets again. This went on for as long as I could remember. Her mother eventually committed her to a drug rehabilitation

1177: Undaunted

program. Mae completed the program and went back home to the Bahamas.

Now Kenneth was the family member that lived with us the longest. He was the cousin I spoke of that drove my dad crazy because he'd park his big ass work truck in our yard. Kenneth was wider than he was tall and had a very serious demeanor. He hardly ever cracked a smile. During the time he lived with us, he worked for Circle K as a store manager, I believe. We would always see him walking toward the house from 17th Avenue, just like Mae had. At first sight, everyone would yell, "There go Kennit"—for some reason, we couldn't pronounce Kenneth—and break off running into the house. We were obviously afraid of him. He held no punches and was not afraid to beat us. Well, let me correct myself and say he wasn't afraid to beat my younger siblings. Whenever I had a problem with one of the boys, all I had to do was tell Kenneth and he would get them in line. Although he was as mean as a pit bull, Kenneth did his best looking after us. Occasionally, he would cook. He'd always call me to the kitchen so I could improve my already existing skills. He was actually the person that taught me that spaghetti was a very inexpensive meal that could be stretched for days.

Chapter

Jo & Co.

She was short and stout with a curly perm. When I think of her, I envision the one picture Babalu had of her sitting at the bar and wearing a teal polo-styled shirt and acid wash jeans. She sat with her legs crossed, posing as if she were Tyra Banks. Her name was Jo and she was Babalu's newest girlfriend. She lived in a duplex that was about a block away from the Banana Boat. She had three children: Jason, Tangie, and Frank. We spent a lot of time at Jo's house. Someone must have chastised Babalu for constantly leaving us home alone. Our experiences there were abusive and tortuous. Jason and Frank would do some of the worst things to us, including waking us from our sleep to blow crushed red pepper into our eyes. Subjecting us to such situations was not only cruel but also more neglectful than any of our prior experiences.

Jason had a girlfriend that he would beat up on a regular basis, and Frank was a hotheaded drug dealer who was more than disrespectful to his mother. And then there was Tangie, Jo's only daughter. She wasn't a part of the shenanigans at the house, likely because she was in a serious relationship with one of the butchers at the local meat market. They had the cutest little boy. His dad's Puerto Rican heritage had given him thick, curly hair that laid against the creamy brown skin his mother had passed on.

Tangie soon became aware of my child-rearing capabilities and before long she was asking me to babysit. Initially her requests were okay—an hour here and there to run to the grocery store. And then shit started getting ridiculous. I remember an occasion when I had to babysit her son *and* her homegirls' kids while they went out partying. I watched the kids at Tangie's apartment. Her place was unfurnished, so we all slept on the floor—well, at least the kids did. I stayed up all night looking out the window and wondering when God was going to save me from the misery I was experiencing.

Chapter

54th Street

I mentioned early on that Babalu was an awesome cook. On a regular basis he'd prepare food for his customers. Hallmark dishes included fried fish, peas and rice, souse, and conch salad. His fish was always seasoned to perfection. He would pour salt and hot peppers into a saucer and then squeeze fresh lime on top. Then, he'd take a spoon and mash everything together until the peppers were pulverized. The seasoning would go over the already cleaned and gutted fish. He would also rub some within the signature slits he always made on each side of the fish's body. And the final touch was the remaining lime juice that he would squeeze over the whole fish, as it awaited its final destination—hot grease. Babalu never coated his fish with flour. He didn't think it was necessary and would curse you out for suggesting it.

His conch salad was the best, though. The conch was always fresh because his aunt would bring him a dozen or two when she visited from the Bahamas. In addition to conch, the salad called for bell pepper, tomato, onion, celery, fresh lime juice, and pepper—usually goat pepper. I imagine the time it took to make conch salad was what caused Babalu to teach us to make it. And before we knew it, we were the conch salad laborers. We would stand up at the very end of the bar and cut up vegetables until our little fingers were wrinkled. This was even more laborious because he wanted the veggies to be cut finely. And he was so serious about that. From time to time, he would check our progress and if he saw vegetables that were larger than his liking, he'd give us a nice tongue lashing, directing us to do as we were told. Unlike the vegetables, the conch had to be cut into medium-size pieces. This was to satisfy customers while also making the conch "stretch." The goat peppers were the worst, though. We'd forget that we cut them with our bare hands and rub our eyes—the burn was serious. And after all of that work, Babalu would only allow each of us a quarter of a tiny cup of conch salad to share. Noticing the pissed off looks on our faces, he'd say, "This ain't for ya'll to eat, this for my customers."

The Banana Boat was surround by Burger King, Popeye's, and a Chinese restaurant, the name of which I can't remember. As all children do, we loved Burger King. We could smell the aroma of the flame-grilled burgers and see its smoky byproducts from the roof. We wanted it even more because it sat directly across from the Banana Boat. Babalu would almost never buy Burger King, though. I guess it was too expensive. Our only saving grace was when "burger buddies" would come out. He would give me four dollars to buy four. If you remember, they were miniature hamburgers (or cheeseburgers) that

54th Street

came in sets of two. We would each have one half of the burger buddy.

We would also eat from Popeye's. I think it was our second favorite. He'd send me to order an eight-piece, mixed. So, I'd probably get two breasts, two legs, two thighs, and two wings. Everyone would get one piece of chicken. And I am embarrassed to admit that the pieces of chicken my siblings got were in concert with their ages. Needless to say, the younger kids got a terrible deal. The upside was that we shared the four biscuits that came along with the chicken, so at least they would have a carbohydrate, providing them some degree of satiety. Anyone who knows anything about Popeye's biscuits knows that they are more than filling.

Our best meal came from the Chinese restaurant, though. I know you're thinking that we liked it the most because of its addictive rice—nope. We loved Chinese food because we could get a bucket of ham fried rice for about ten dollars. The bucket would allow everyone to get large portions and have enough for seconds.

To date, all of those restaurants remain on 54th Street and 7th Avenue, including the Banana Boat (now called Shantel). Each time I ride down that street I can still feel our presence.

Not long after Babalu moved the Banana Boat, he moved us. He'd settled us in a house on 54th Street and 10th Avenue. Like our previous house, it was old and wooden, but this one actually sat on bricks. The house had three bedrooms, one bathroom, and a den that no one wanted to sit in. The front and back yards had more dirt than grass, and I could always hear something running around within the roof. I assumed it was a possum or a big ass rat. The neighborhood was pretty quiet, though. It was during this time we began to see Ya-Yow again. Now homeless and pregnant, she would pop up to the house out of nowhere. You could hear her before you saw her. As she approached our house, she'd scream one of our names from the top of her lungs. Excitedly, we'd run outside to see what she wanted. I believe she missed us.

Ya-Yow would always smell like pee. So the first thing we made her do was take a bath. Because of her height, we didn't have much to offer her in terms of clothing. But we made do with what we had. I would also comb her hair. Despite being homeless, her hair was never matted. It was actually clean—for the most part. I would part her hair in fours and give her four dukie plaits, just like she preferred. Before she left, she would always make sure she took something to remember us by. Ya-Yow would take socks, shirts, combs—you name it and she took it. She even took one of the lace gloves I had worn to my middle school prom. I can still see her walking down the street with the glove on her left hand. Onlookers likely viewed her strangely, wondering why she was wearing a single lace glove. But I saw her as a mother who missed her kids, and if a lace glove would keep her close to them, then so be it.

After Shadeaw, Ya-Yow gave birth to two more children, bringing her to a total of thirteen. The second to last child was a girl she named Teri in honor of her eldest brother. Because Ya-Yow was homeless when she had Teri, she had to give her up. Babalu was next of kin, so naturally he would be the one Teri was given to. Well aware of his existing predicament, Babalu gave Teri to *his* eldest son, Eddie, and Eddie's wife at the time. I don't know if they formally adopted her because Teri kept my mother's last name, Buford. Eddie and his wife raised Teri together in Miami until their divorce. Thereafter, his wife moved back to the Bahamas and took Teri with her. We wouldn't see her again for years.

Ya-Yow's last child, a boy, was also born while she was homeless. He was immediately adopted after birth. Not long ago, I asked a friend of mine who worked for the Department of Children and Families (DCF) to look him up and she was able to find him. A grown man now, "Michael" is somewhere out there, unaware that he has twelve sisters and brothers.

Chapter

11

"God Is Love"

After Michael was born, Ya-Yow came to visit us again. For some reason, she wanted take a trip to the Banana Boat—and we had to go with her. My youngest brother Eddie, also known as Lil Eddie, was reluctant to go so she had to drag him by his ear. Ha! As we were walking I could see a woman standing to my right. She was having a conversation with another woman while watching us walk down the street. There were numerous people on the street that day, but this lady stood out for some reason. It was as if we were supposed to cross paths. About a week after that encounter, Babalu announced that we would be going to church and to be ready when our ride came to pick us up. We were all confused. Church? Up to this point, we had never spoken of church, let alone attended a service. Sunday morning soon came and I had everyone ready. We didn't have much in the way of clothing, but I made the best of what we had. Bodies were bathed, clothes were ironed, and hair was combed. I didn't know who was coming to pick us up, but we were definitely going to present our best to them.

We sat patiently, waiting for the "mystery people"

to arrive. And then we heard the sound of a loud horn. Wanting to confirm the call was for us, I had everyone wait. And then the driver blew the horn a second time. I directed everyone to go outside. And as I closed the door behind me, I looked up and saw a doo-doo brown van parked outside of our house. There was a fair-skinned woman with a big grin on her face, looking as if she was happy to see us. Her teeth were perfect, and as I got closer to her, I could see that she either had dentures or a permanent implant. I sat in the front seat and everyone else sat in the row of seats immediately behind me—except rather than car seats, there were chairs that obviously meant to replace the standard second row of seating. And off we went.

"God Is Love Prayer and Mission Center" (God Is Love) was painted on the front of the all white building that was about as big as the house we lived in. We entered through the back door and to our left was the sanctuary. It was filled with cranberry-colored pews settled in the middle and on each side of the room. A drum set and organ sat in the far right-hand corner. We took our seats and what I came to know as "devotion" began. Three women stood before us, asking everyone to stand. There wasn't a musical set nor were there any "real" musicians like we see in our churches today. The members were the musicians. The ladies that stood before us sang, and a teenage boy, whom I later learned was named Antwan, played the drums. Antwan was the neighbor of God Is Love's assistant pastor, Sister Grace. She was the one who picked us up that morning and every other morning thereafter. Antwan was more than dark-skinned, like blue-black. His lips and nose were just as noticeable as the darkness of his skin. He was always accompanied by his baby sister, whose name I cannot remember. But after only moments with them, you knew that he would rather leave her at home. She was whiney and always in need of him.

Antwan's drum playing proved that he had on-the-job training. His cadence was nothing more than *boom-tat, boom-tat, boom-tat, boom-boom-tat* to "I don't know what you come to do, Oooh, I don't know what you come to do." The congregation would repeat the devotion leaders' lyrics, which usually involved an action. "I come to clap my hands—my hands, I come to stump my feet—my feet, I come to stump my feet—my feet, I come to do my dance—my dance." And at any point during the song, the leader could repeat the action over and over and over and over again. They were usually "in the spirit" by then.

It was like nothing I had experienced before. People were clapping, jumping up and down, playing the tambourine, and even beating on the back of the wooden pews in front of them. And after devotion was over, the floor would be opened up for testimonies. During this time the most grateful would stand before the congregation and talk about how good God had been to them. People were generally grateful for things like waking up in the morning, their children, and the ability to open their mouths and thank Him. And then there were people who had very specific things they were thankful for. This could be a new job, unexpected money, or even saving their lives.

1177: Undaunted

My favorite was Sister Cheryl. She stood about 5' tall and had the cutest, tiniest hands and feet you could imagine. Her skin was like smooth milk chocolate and she had long thick, shiny black hair. She was married to Bob, a Jamaican that probably failed P.E. because he was so serious. Like Cheryl, Bob was short but had an unforgettable presence. Cheryl and Bob had three children: a set of twin boys named James and Jeremiah, and a daughter named Prima. We rarely saw Bob, though. Cheryl and the kids usually attended service without him. But when he did attend, we knew it was an act of God. Sister Cheryl's testimonies would always be preceded by song. She had a strong alto-tenor voice that carried beyond the doors of the church. She sang with passion—eyes closed, heart and spirit open. You could tell that life was hard for her, but she always pressed through. Her faith made her strong and you could hear it when she sang.

While everyone was singing and dancing, I saw her again. There she was, the lady I'd seen only weeks prior standing in her yard as we passed with Ya-Yow! Her name was Sarah—Sister Sarah—and she was God Is Love's pastor. She walked from behind a door that was a part of a room connected to the pulpit. I soon learned that the room was her office. She joined everyone in devotion—clapping, singing, and playing the tambourine. She could do the latter like no other. I noticed her looking out into the congregation, likely for us. And after spotting our faces, she smiled. I guess she was worried that we wouldn't make it to service. It was only a few years ago that I learned that Sister Sarah ran into my dad at the nearby meat market (the same one where

"God Is Love"

Tangie's boyfriend worked) and, for some reason, she asked him if we were his kids. Their conversation ended with him agreeing to let us go to church with her.

Once devotion was over, she stepped up to the podium, greeted everyone, and started praying. Her alto voice was palpable. You could feel it in your soul. And although I wasn't supposed to, I opened my eyes to get another peek at the woman that would have a major part in changing my life forever. With her eyes closed tightly, feet fixed and forehead wrinkled, Sister Sarah prayed as if she were standing before God. Her requests to Him were preceded by words of thanks and gratefulness—showing appreciation for all he had done for her. And when she was finally done, everyone's voice would be lifted up in praise—"touching and agreeing" with every word Sister Sarah uttered.

Before then, I had never seen or heard a woman preaching. The only thing I'd seen woman do professionally was teach. I was in awe. Soon after that visit, we became members of God Is Love. On Tuesdays we attended bible study, and on Wednesdays we had a normal service. Youth choir rehearsal was held on Thursdays—I don't believe there was a youth choir until we showed up—hell, we just about made up the entire choir. And Saturday mornings would be dedicated to cleaning in preparation for Sunday morning service.

I began to enjoy church. I really can't explain why. Maybe because it got me out of the house or maybe because of the people—Sisters Sarah and

Cheryl. I don't know. Maybe it had something to do with the routine it provided me. For the first time in my life I had something to look forward to besides school. And as time went on, my "like" for it turned into "love." I paid attention in bible study, taking notes so that I had something to refer to during the week when I needed inspiration. And every once in a while, I'd be allowed to lead devotion. That was always exciting. Although my vocals were not the best, I was never coy about using them. I also became quite the tambourine player, and I didn't mind standing up to testify about how awesome God had been. I even spoke in "tongues." Repeating what I'd seen and heard from the elders of the church, I'd belt out a "Shamdula-Shaamma" or a "Hashura-Bo." To date, India and Simone still make fun of me for that. During the many times we'd reminisce about the "good old days," one or the other of them would stand up and ask, "Remember when Charkes used to speak in tongues? She'd stand up with her eyes closed, rub her hands together, and be saying 'Hundala-Shaam' and 'Isiro-Coo.' And we'd be looking at her like, 'girl what the hell you saying?'" And once the instant replay was over, everyone would bust out laughing, including me.

But the thing that was most important was my salvation. Yes, I got "saved." Although unconscious of what was actually happening, things seemed to get better for us after we met Sister Sarah. And because she was a pastor, I was more than convinced that she was an act of God. So, I gave my life to Him.

"God Is Love"

In addition to the spiritual food she provided, Sister Sarah fed us physically. If we weren't eating Palm supermarket's fried chicken dinners at church (usually after service), we were sitting in front of plates of food piled high from Sadie's Buffet, our favorite eating spot. After service, Sister Sarah would announce that we were going to Sadie's, at which point, everyone would have to decide which Buford they would be sponsoring. As you can imagine, feeding eight children is costly. We'd be super excited, though. Not only because we were getting a full meal, but also because we could fill our bellies with all of the ice cream our hearts desired. Immediately after finishing our dinner, we'd run over to the ice cream dispenser and fill the beige plastic-porcelain bowls with strawberry, vanilla, and chocolate ice cream—or maybe a combination of all three. And how could I forget the nuts, strawberries, caramel, and fudge we used to top our treats. Needless to say, our drive home was quiet. Like most who consume large amounts of food and then have to sit for long periods of time afterward, we all suffered from the "itis."

Turned out, "the Bufords," as we were affectionately called, weren't the only heartbroken and heavy-laden folks Sister Sarah had discovered and taken in. There were at least a half dozen other people with stories similar to ours, and for some reason, they also crossed Sister Sarah's path. Like she did for us, she fed (physically and spiritually) and clothed them. She even housed some. Sister Sarah was an anomaly.

Although many called her "mom," Sister Sarah only had one biological child, Jackie. Everyone knew her as Jack. Jack must have been in her early twenties when we met. She was voluptuous, and her face was pretty, just like her smile. But nothing stood out more than her hearty laugh. Whenever she had a sweet joke, she'd belt one out, automatically making you do the same. She would always place her hand over her mouth, attempting to muffle the sound. And when things got really funny, you'd see tears running from her eyes. Just writing about her makes me laugh.

Like I had with Angie, I immediately took to Jack. Despite her being the youth choir director, she was really cool. Jack lived in a two-bedroom apartment in the back of Sister Sarah's house. It was small and quaint. The unused kitchen was tiny, but the remainder of the place had normal-size rooms. The kitchen was noticeable because it was the first thing you saw upon entering her apartment. She had a roommate, Tina. Tina was a member of God is Love as well, and if I remember correctly, she was also the cousin of one of Sister Sarah's best friends. Tina was quiet—the total opposite of Jack. She was tall for a woman, thinly framed, and had medium-brown skin. She also had the silkiest hair. Like us, Tina had a troubled family. She had a homosexual brother, who died of AIDS years later (with Sister Sarah by his side), and she had a sister who was addicted to drugs, precluding her responsibilities as a mother. Despite all, Tina remained faithful to God. Her disposition was one of gratefulness and humility; you felt it in her testimonies and saw it in her daily walks—she was committed to Him.

"God Is Love"

And then there was Toni. Toni was one of the broken hearted and heavy laden folk I mentioned earlier. Toni was short, brown-skinned. and had a medium build. Her personality was framed in cockiness while her core was one of insecurity. At first glance, anyone could tell she was unsure of herself—even I could see that at such an early age. She was obviously a girl, but had a "boyish" side to her that she seemed very comfortable with. Wearing baggy shorts, oversized T-shirts, and sneakers was effortless for her, while donning a dress on Sunday mornings was an arduous task. I guess that was the driving force in her and Sister Sarah's relationship—confusion and uncertainty. I was never very fond of Toni. And the fact that she was sneaking around with my man intensified those feelings. We'll get to that later. From time to time, Toni would also stay at Jack's place. We all enjoyed being there—talking, singing, and joking around. Being at Jack's made me feel like a teenager and I imagine it provided Tina and Toni a degree of solace as well.

Kevin was the nephew of Sister Sarah's close friend Caro, who preferred to be called Jo. Early on, I learned that Jo was homosexual. And although I never saw her with a woman, she fit the script. She was masculine and always wore pants, except for when she went to church. And even then, she'd wear a very basic skirt suit. Her thick, jet-black hair was cut close—and the top was only inches long. Her thirty-two teeth sat perfectly in her mouth, including the sole gold-plated one. She drove an older model Chevy Corvette that was almost black and had seats that were worn and cracked. But her greatest identifier was her employment. Jo worked

1177: Undaunted

in the deli at Palm supermarket. Because of her, our Sunday dinners would be filled with all of the fried chicken we could stand. And you know how everybody loves "Palm fried chicken."

Kevin and I met for the first time in the back of God Is Love's van—the van that picked us up for church every Sunday morning. Not long after we met, we became girlfriend and boyfriend. Because I was only thirteen, and he was fifteen, we had to be secretive about our relationship. But despite our secrecy, Sister Sarah eventually got word of what was going on. Surprisingly, she never reprimanded me. I guess she trusted Kevin and me to do the right thing.

Kevin was not only my first boyfriend but he was also my first love. I was naturally attracted to him. He was tall, dark, and handsome with eyes that were almond shaped and piercing. His lips were big and soft and always wet. I guess you want to know how I knew so much about his lips, huh? Needless to say, Kevin and I used the back of the van as our kissing booth. He taught me how to kiss. Not caring that the other kids on the bus would catch us, we'd lip-lock at first sight of one another. Whenever I knew he was visiting Sister Sarah, I'd conveniently find my way to her house. Wearing what I considered my best outfit and my hair styled like Lisa from the Cult Jam, I'd walk over to Sister Sarah's, which was only a block away. No, let me take that back, I probably skipped over there while singing Cheryl Lynn's "Love Come Down"! Upon appearing on her doorstep, she'd shout "Hooooney," while laughing at

"God Is Love"

the same time—letting me know that she knew why I was there.

Kevin and I would also meet up at Jack's house. This would always be a planned event. Because he didn't have a car, Kevin would usually get a ride from one of his friends, which was convenient because someone would always be interested in hooking up with Jack or Toni. Initially, we'd all sit around talking about the latest events, church, and relationships—whatever came to mind. And then everyone would eventually end up in his or her own quarters, leaving Kevin and me in the living room. We would kiss, rub, and dry hump until our hearts were content. And even though he probably wanted to do more, Kevin always remained a gentleman. He never pressured me into doing more than he knew I could handle.

Our relationship continued until I found out he was cheating on me with Toni. They forged a relationship right underneath my nose! I got word that they skipped school one day, meeting at his place in the Clover Leaf apartments. I felt more than betrayed—I was heartbroken. And at thirteen years old, I got my first dose of what I would continuously experience as an adult: disappointment courtesy of a man I had fallen in love with. Kevin eventually had four kids, got married, and then divorced. And I hear he recently got married again. In our adult life we toyed with the idea of attempting another romantic relationship, but it never felt right to me. I'd rather remain friends—that was more important. Despite all, Kevin will always be my "first love."

CHAPTER

"INNER CITY"

As a child, Jack danced for Inner City Children's Touring Dance Company (ICCTDC), a dance troupe located in the heart of Liberty City, Florida, otherwise known as "the City." The troupe was founded by Florene Litthcut Nichols. Jack must have only danced for a short period of time because I never saw any recital pictures of her during her teenage years. Her pictures were limited to when she was six and seven years old—you know, the ones you see in every parent's living room, sitting on a coffee table. One day, out of nowhere, Sister Sarah told us that we would be taking dance lessons at ICCTDC. Dance lessons? I thought. I think I was just as stunned as when Babalu told us we were going to church. And the following week, the three of us took the first of many walks to 43rd Street and 7th Avenue.

We walked into the studio and were greeted by a woman we came to know as Ms. Duncan. Ms. Duncan was Ms. Nichols's assistant and she was always the first face you saw when you walked in. She asked who we were and my reply—"Charkes Nesbitt, India Buford, and Simone Buford"—must have reminded her of something pleasant because she was grinning from ear to ear. After our brief conversation, she moved from the back of her workstation and went to get Ms. Nichols. Within seconds I saw a woman standing before me who was nothing short of fierce—she was beautiful. Standing about 5' 6" tall, she had blemishless, latte-colored skin that protected a set of high cheekbones that made her look like a supermodel. She hugged us (as she always come to do), and soon after, her tender, soft face turned into a stern one. Immediately, she told us what classes we would be taking and the days we needed to be in attendance. She was firm and direct in making us aware that being a part of ICCTDC was a privilege and that we were to show our appreciation by coming to class on time and in appropriate attire. Agreeing, I shook my head and said yes at the same time. India and Simone did the same. We were beyond excited. And the next four to eight years of our lives would be filled with tap, ballet, West African, and Dunham-style dancing— all free of charge.

The studio sat (and still does) on the corner of 43rd Street and 7th Avenue. If you travel south on 7th Avenue, you will see the building on the right, just as you approach the overpass. As soon as you walked in the studio, the smell of incense would hit you. I never knew if Ms. Nichols was burning incense or if she used a special air freshener, but the aroma of plants combined with oil was unforgettable. You could smell it in her clothes and in her house. Ms. Duncan's workstation sat on the left, and along the right side of the building were the dance rooms, except for our Dunham classroom—it was on the

"Inner City"

left. All of the floors were hardwood, and mirrors took up every inch of wall space.

My African dance teacher was a thick, short, dark-complexioned woman with a "natural" appearance. She looked as if her house was lined with incense, African prints, and Congo drums. Her name was Alice— Ms. Alice to us. In addition to a black leotard and tights, Ms. Alice made us wear Lapas. Lapas are pieces of printed cloth traditionally worn in African dance ceremonies. Those of us that had voluptuous rear ends would wrap our Lapas as tight as we could so that our pubescent asses would be noticed. And then we'd spend at least two to three minutes in the mirror, admiring our reflections. Ms. Alice would always have to call our names, directing us to get away from the mirror and line up for class.

African class was my favorite. I liked it most because of its energy, which came from the live drum. It was the soul of the technique; there is no dance without it. At the sound of the very first drumbeat, you were connected—it made you feel like you were in Ghana, dancing among your family as a rite of passage. The movements were combinations of thrusts, jerks, and stomps, performed precisely and quickly—all at the same time. The drums usually took the lead. And while dancing, you'd have to keep a keen ear because at any point during your performance, a "drum break" would come, alerting you to change your move. This was different from most styles of dance as it allowed a certain freedom while still being controlled by the drum. Class usually began with single-move floor exercises that, by the end of class, were grouped to form choreography.

Dunham is an Afro-Caribbean-American style of dance created by Katherine Dunham (1909–2006). Also a social anthropologist, Katherine Dunham used dance to give voice to African-based social and cultural rituals. During the 1940s, she founded the first African-American dance school, maintaining it for close to thirty years. Ms. Eaton taught Dunham, and from what I've learned about the creator of the dance style, Ms. Eaton was more than fitting as an instructor. Now, Ms. Eaton wasn't exactly what you'd envision when you thought of a dance teacher. She was overweight, which in some cases precludes one's ability to dance—at least professionally. But that didn't make one bit of a difference. Her weight never kept her from moving like butter. With legs stretched high, her arms extended, and her back perfectly arched, it was obvious she had dedicated her life to dance, including the Dunham technique.

And then there was my tap teacher, Carmen, who preferred to be called Tina. "Tina" was an abbreviated version of her middle name, Catina. Carmen was one of Ms. Nichols's protégés. She'd been a part of ICCTDC for more than a decade and was considered one of its best dancers. Carmen was beautiful and had a body every teenage girl would die for—well, back then at least. Her chest was flat and her tummy even flatter. Her greatest assets were her perfectly shaped legs—scarless and always clean shaven. And although grown by the time I reached ICCTDC, she had the face of a teenage girl. Carmen was always serious, though. She never cracked a

"Inner City"

smile. I guess she had to position herself that way in order for us to take her and her class seriously. I still remember some of the things she taught me: side slaps, front slaps, time steps, and dig-spank-heel-sa-lap heel. You would practice the former just as I typed it, using the opposite foot to execute the heel part of the technique. Carmen and I eventually became friends and remain so to this day.

The exposure we got at ICCTDC was irreplaceable. Not only did we learn to dance, but we also learned that there was life outside of the walls Babalu had created for us. We performed at events with audiences that included congressmen, mayors, and other city officials who made financial investments to ICCTDC—giving underprivileged girls like myself an opportunity. Ms. Nichols also spent time with us outside of the studio. She would invite Company members—that is, students who performed throughout the year—over to her house for dinner. This would always be a big deal because it meant we'd receive etiquette training while dining. She'd usually prepare a huge meal and formally set her dining room table, making sure there was a place for each and every one of us. We usually enjoyed two to three courses, and for each one, we had to know which spoon and fork to use and which side of the plate to place our drinking glass. And you had better not put both hands on the dining room table. You had to decide which hand you would use to eat and which would be placed on your lap throughout dinner, with the exception of using it to wipe excess food or drink from your mouth. Ms. Nichols was well known and had more than infiltrated Miami-Dade County, which meant that we would be

1177: Undaunted

introduced to people who thought table manners and politeness were important. I'm forever grateful for those lessons. Had it not been for Ms. Nichols, I honestly do not know how or when I would have learned them.

Ms. Nichols would also take us to Bayside, which was always fun. Bayside was—and still is—one of Miami's main attractions. Now settled right next to the American Airlines Arena, Bayside attracted all who wanted to shop, eat, and listen to live music—all while overlooking Miami's bay. It was, and remains, beautiful. We'd walk around, enjoying the sites, and we would always top our outing off with virgin piña coladas. She loved them.

And because of Ms. Nichols, I attended my first and only high school football game, known as the "Soul Bowl," shopped at Cache at her expense, learned to apply makeup, and took my first trip out of the country.

In the summer of 1989, Inner City Children's Touring Dance Company was asked to perform at the World's Fair—and guess where—in Seville, Spain! I couldn't believe it. Outside of going to the Bahamas to see my cousins, I hadn't traveled anywhere outside of the Miami-Dade County line, which is to say that I was more than excited about the trip. I don't remember asking Babalu if I could go. It didn't matter anyway, because I was going regardless of what he said. I hardly ever sought his approval or asked his permission for anything, I just did it. And if there were something that required a signature, I'd just forge it. I imagine that's how I was able to

"Inner City"

get a passport. The cost of the trip was free for me with the exception of clothes and spending money, all of which Sister Sarah took care of. To date, she reminds me of how she took up a collection for me at her job at North Shore Hospital and how there was a particular doctor who made a very sizeable donation. If by chance that doctor is reading this, thank you!

Before I knew it, I was standing in Miami International Airport in my black and purple Nike sweat suit—our travel uniform. Naturally, a lot of the girls' parents took advantage of the trip. I distinctly remember Mashinda's mom and dad. They stuck out because they were so in love. I still hold a picture in my mind of her mom lying on her dad's lap, fast asleep while waiting for our bus to take us to the performance site. With envy, I admired how he stroked her head, as I wondered why Ya-Yow and Babalu didn't have that type of relationship.

My adrenaline overshadowed the protracted trip. The twelve-hour flight seemed to take only thirty minutes and I was wide awake the entire time. I didn't want to miss a thing. As we prepared to land, I opened my window to get a view of the country. Those views are always the best, no matter where you're landing. I recall mountainous land with square houses settled up high and down low—much different from what I saw in Liberty City. Clearing customs and getting to our living quarters made our first day seem longer than the plane ride there. Our mornings were filled with rehearsals—for hours we prepared for our daily scheduled performances. But showtime made every minute of rehearsal worth it.

1177: Undaunted

At the beginning of each piece, you could feel the crowd's amazement—it was almost palpable. The audiences comprising of thousands of people stood to their feet in awe as we—foreigners to them—performed hip-hop, Caribbean, and tap pieces. And they showed their amazement through the eruption of applause at the end.

The most memorable time in Spain was taking a trip over to Morocco, Africa. Yes, we went to AFRICA! Ms. Nichols took us there during the latter portion of our trip—it was a treat for performing so well. And again, she wanted to provide us a "once in a lifetime" type of experience. As we entered a Moroccan restaurant, we were greeted in the most jovial manner. There were people standing at the restaurant's entrance, smiling from ear to ear, all while shaking our hands. Before being seated, we had to remove our shoes and place them neatly in the front corner of the room we were dining in. I assume this was Moroccan tradition. I was afraid to do so, fearing someone might see my feet and make fun of my toes. Those that know me best are probably laughing hard as hell reading this because they would immediately get a visual of my toes, which are reminiscent of Fred Flintstone's toes. After removing our shoes, we sat in an Indian-style position on the carpeted floor and indulged in a traditional Moroccan meal. Okay, I just ramped you up and you are now expecting detail, right? However, the only detail I have is that the food was spicy as hell. More spice than I was used to, despite exposure to such in Bahamian dishes. We dared not complain, though. Ms. Nichols would have been displeased and you didn't want those problems. Furthermore,

"Inner City"

the opportunity I was afforded by attending this trip precluded gripes about how spicy my meal was. So my lips were sealed. On the way back to Seville, I stood aside from everyone else, enjoying the water, enjoying the air—enjoying the things that were not available to me in the city that awaited my return.

Chapter 13

The "Scotts"

My final residence before leaving Miami was "the projects"—that is, the James E. Scott Projects. Spanning from 73rd Street to 79th Street, and around 19th Avenue to about 24th Avenue, the projects are a direct reflection of its name. Owned by the government, the projects were lower-income houses that theoretically provided "a means to an end," but actually only provided "an end" for the families housed there. Of course, all who found habitation in the projects were economically disadvantaged, which in most instances is synonymous with being a racial minority. Single women headed all households—well, at least until we moved into the neighborhood. The buildings were stacked like dominoes, in rows. Each building would house anywhere from three to eight families. We moved to the projects about a year before I went to Spain, in 1991.

Immediately, I was shocked. Although the neighborhoods we lived in prior to moving to the projects weren't the best of the best, they were definitely better. The projects had a community within itself, one whose government was comprised of drug dealers and "watch out boys." The drug dealers supervised and manned the "drug holes," which were areas within the projects where drugs were sold. Coincidentally, the area and its name represent the same thing—emptiness. The drug hole in closest proximity to us was "P.E.," which was short for Public Enemy. Although P.E.'s main product was weed, I would often see users departing with cocaine and crack. I knew this because from time to time I would either stand peeping from our screened front door or the upstairs window—the one from which my siblings had managed to permanently remove the screen. At times, patrons would be so eager to enjoy their purchase they'd get high right in front of our house.

Supporting the drug dealers, were the watch out boys. These people, usually boys, would stand or sit on a milk crate on the corner, looking for police. This position was important because being caught with marijuana, crack, or cocaine in Florida could cost you the rest of your life in prison. Once cited, they'd yell "nine in the hole" or "nine on"— whichever street and avenue the police were last seen on. Hearing that police were approaching or in the hole would cause drug dealers to flee immediately. When the coast was clear, the watch out boy would yell, "outta der," meaning the police were gone and no longer a threat.

There were times when watch out boys weren't able to protect their domains from police, though. And those times were when "jump out" visited. "Jump out" were undercover police officers posing as civilians in order to slickly raid drug holes and

The "Scotts"

arrest anyone in close proximity. A jump out visit usually resulted in an arrest or two. Residents of the projects had to be very careful during these times because drug dealers would run into their houses attempting to hide themselves and their dope from police. And if by chance a drug dealer was followed into someone's home, anything found could be put on the lessee, risking an eviction.

I soon found myself "crushing" on "Heat," one of the P.E. drug dealers. Not much older than me, Heat was a child selling drugs. He and his younger siblings lived across the street from us in what we called the "new projects." Day and night, Heat worked in P.E., looking to make sure he had the means to support his family and wear the best of the best. He eventually recognized that I liked him. I guess he noticed me staring at him from afar, out of our bedroom window. Like most Miamians, he loved the University of Miami (UM) football team. I knew this because he wore their paraphernalia often. I don't know how, but I patched up enough money to buy him a UM fitted cap. I'd gotten it from the USA Flea Market—one of the only places to shop nearby. I was extremely nervous about giving it to him, and when I finally conjured up enough nerve to do so, I was disappointed. Standing on our front porch, I made eye contact with him and beckoned him to walk over to our house. As I saw him approaching, I stepped off of the porch to meet him on the sidewalk. I think he could see that I'd bought something for him because he was smiling, showing all ten of his gold teeth. I opened the small, white plastic bag, removed the orange and green hat, and handed it to him. All at once, he took the hat out of my hand and placed it on his head—he seemed impressed by my gesture of kindness, which communicated my like for him. And then he dropped the bomb. As sweetly as he could, he said that although he liked me, he wasn't good for me. In agreeance, but crushed at the same time, I walked away. Months after, I would still watch him from our bedroom window, hoping and wishing he'd change his mind.

Chapter 14

G. Holmes Braddock

Although I had gotten used to the dysfunction of the projects, I never succumbed to the standard culture or mindset. I was hell-bent on setting myself apart from those I sympathized and empathized with. Initially, I secluded myself, only coming out to walk to the bus stop for school or to the Arab-owned corner store. The more people acknowledged my difference, the more I wanted to be different. At times, I would purposely sit in the living room and do my homework, waiting for someone to see my head buried in a book, knowing something would be said. Once I heard someone say, "Oh, look at her, she so smart," or "That's good, girl, do your work," I'd raise my head in a surprised fashion, acknowledging their comment while acting as if I hadn't been expecting it. I also prided myself in the fact that I didn't attend the high school I was zoned for, Miami Northwestern Senior High. For three years, at 5 a.m., I would stand on the corner (with whichever dope boy working that night) of 73rd Street and 21st Avenue and await the arrival of the bus to take me to G. Holmes Braddock Senior High, or simply Braddock.

Located at 3601 SW 147th Avenue, Braddock's racial population matched its surrounding neighborhood. The majority of the students were Hispanic and Caucasian, an enrollment that begged for the integration of other cultures and ethnicities. The school needed a little "racial equity." And like most schools with this challenge, Braddock adopted a magnet program. Magnet programs afforded schools the opportunity to attract students of other races and socioeconomic backgrounds. I believe they had a professional magnet program and recruited me for it back when I was at Charles R. Drew Middle School.

Braddock opened its doors in August 1990 and my class was the first to step foot on its grounds. In addition, the freshmen were the first group of students to attend all four years, graduating in 1994. The campus was ginormous, and the courtyard, which was just as big, sat smack dab in the middle of the campus. When I had class on the second floor, I'd always take a little time to look down at the courtyard to watch hundreds of students walking in every direction, trying to get to class. I met some of my best friends at Braddock—Robyne, Chekena (Kena), Michelle, Nacresha (Cresha), Angela (Angie), and Shakesha (Kesha). Like me, they were bussed to Braddock and looking to get away from the mundane experiences of the inner city and its schools. The relationships forged with these young ladies were not only wanted but also needed during that time in my life. They were all special to me, for different reasons.

Kesha and I met by way of her first cousin,

Angie. Kesha was short with a Leisure Curl style and had the cutest face and smoothest skin. She was also an undercover comedian, finding humor in most things, and always laughing at her own jokes. I remember her always covering her mouth with a clenched fist to hide her smile when she laughed. I never understood why she did that, though. Kesha was special because she was like me. Later on in life, she revealed details about abuse and insecurity, an admission that made us kindred spirits. Kesha had a tough cover but nothing but soft sweetness lay underneath—like kiwi fruit. What made her even more special was the fact she would always invite me over to her house. During those times, we'd talk, laugh, and joke around for hours. Kesha was even responsible for me attending my first concert—the Budweiser Superfest. I assume she convinced her folks to buy me a ticket—sort of like what my son Adrian does for friends of his who are less fortunate. I don't know who performed, but I do remember hearing "I Will Always Love You" for the first time, a song that crowned Whitney Houston as the greatest voice of our time.

Angie was the epitome of what every girl wanted to look and feel like. She had latte-colored skin, a wide beautiful smile and the whitest, prettiest teeth, a woman's ass, and killer legs. All of the guys were attracted to her. However, the most beautiful thing about Angie was her personality. Always pleasant and kind, she never let any of her physical beauty get to her head. And through her smile you felt every bit of her spirit. Angie and I were alike in that we loved dance. I believe we shared Mrs. Perry's dance class in the eleventh grade. I'll never forget an assignment we had that required us to choreograph a three-minute piece to the song of our choosing. We chose "Been So Long" by Anita Baker. Only the Lord knows why we chose such a song, but we both loved it. At this moment I'm reminiscing on our practice times—both of us standing outside the dance room in our black leotards and tights while I continuously stared at Angie's body, wishing my little narrow ass could look like hers.

Cresha was special to me because she was the sister of my boyfriend at the time, Jefferson, although everyone knew him as FLIMP, which stood for "Fucking Ladies In Many Positions." Yeah, I know. Why would I date someone with such a name? I never paid any attention to that though. Jefferson lived in the Brown Sub community; a neighborhood filled with violence, drugs, and hopelessness—just like the one I lived in. He was a part of that hopelessness. Jefferson was a drug dealer. But for some reason he gave Braddock a chance. For me that was huge. The fact that he was able to look beyond his situation and attempt to find another lane to live in meant he had potential. Our greatest times together were on the "activity bus". This bus transported students who had afterschool activities back to their homes. We all used the bus, despite our nonexistent afterschool activities. Our rides home would be filled with kissing, hand-holding, and caressing. I believe we both needed that degree of intimacy. It was a way for us to escape our realities—even if it was on a school bus. We'd also talk a lot. Of course, my contributions to the conversation were always about what was going on at home and he'd reciprocate by telling me all about his life crises.

Our lives at that time, however, precluded anything beyond Braddock and the activity bus. He was a new father and had to find a way to make a living to take care of his child. There was no room for me.

Despite my relationship with Jeff, Cresha and I became really good friends. It was easy to be Cresha's friend; she had the coolest demeanor and she was one of the most stylish teenagers I'd ever met. Her long, jet-black hair was always laid and her fingernails always perfectly manicured. She had an innate sense for fashion. Cresha was exceptional in the way she put her outfits together. She always managed to maintain her girlish image while still giving off the edge of a grown woman. Interestingly enough, she now has her very own swimsuit line called Vanae. Cresha and I shared a number of intimacies, including the love she had for a grown man. I knew how they had met, how they spent time together, and all of the stories she made up to tell her mom in order to be with him. I never told a soul, though. I've always believed that my relationships with my friends were *our* relationships and not everyone else's despite how interwoven we all were.

I believe Michelle started Braddock during our tenth grade year. She transferred over from Miami Norland, a high school located in northwest Miami-Dade. Michelle and I were about the same height, weight, and color. Her hair was always pulled into a ponytail, decorated by a bang in the back, front, or both. Most mornings, "T" (a friend of ours) would hot curl her bangs before school started, giving her hairstyle a little personality. I also remember her always wearing this god-awful nylon sweat suit jacket. No matter what the weather, Michelle and that jacket were always together. And when it got too hot, she'd just tie it around her waist, like some sort of ornament. Michelle briefly dated Jefferson's brother, Corey. While Michelle was "the girl next door," he was the "bad boy." So we often referred to them as "Whitney and Bobby"—their relationship was just as unlikely as the celebrities'. Michelle and I eventually became distant, though. To make a long story short—her boyfriend and I were not as compatible as we were. But as God will have it, Michelle and I reunited two years ago and are now thick as thieves. Her ex-boyfriend and I forged a friendship as well.

Kena, Robyne, and I were the closest in the group. I assume because we were tough and didn't take anybody's shit. Well, at least Kena and I didn't. Kena was tall for a girl and already shaped like a woman. She was extremely smart and always seemed to make good decisions. For instance, both of us became nurses, but Kena seemed to have known this was her calling way before I did. In our Advanced Placement literature class, I clearly remember her saying that she would attend Florida State University (FSU) and major in nursing. I, on the other hand, had no idea about what I was going to do with my life. My only verbal commitment to a career was when I once said I wanted to be a waitress—and that was because I used to watch *Mel's Diner* on TV all the time. It wasn't until my sophomore year at Bethune-Cookman College (BCC) that I made a decision, and the reasoning behind that was security. Nursing seemed safe. I would always have a job and the pay was good. And aside from dancing, I had no other interests. But I wasn't good enough at that to make it a career—I'd started too late and had already reached my peak. Well, at least that's what I thought.

Kena also had a boyfriend, "Boo." He was a grown man—nothing like the rooty-poot guys Robyne and I were dating. I believe he had already graduated from high school and was preparing to serve in the U.S. Marines. Kena and Boo were in love and it was clear that they would spend the rest of their lives together. Just about every day, I'd have to sit and listen to Kena go on and on about their dates, what he had brought for her, and how they were going to get married. What was most interesting about their relationship was the fact that Kena's mom would let Boo spend the night. To me, that was unheard of. In our house, Babalu made it clear that boys were the enemy and we weren't to look at them, think of them, or even speak to them. And during the times you were able to sneak and call your little boyfriend, you'd better make the conversation quick. Because once Babalu found out you were on the phone, all hell would break loose. I'd get a "Get your fuckin ass off this phone." So Kena's situation amazed me. It spoke of her mother's liberal way of thinking, Kena's maturity, and the trusting relationship they had. Kena and Boo eventually got married, had two children (a boy and girl), and now live in Arizona. A couple of years ago, Boo retired from the Marines and is now part-owner of a successful coffee company. Kena went on to become a family nurse practitioner, and guess what, their daughter is now studying to be a registered nurse.

Robyne was the life of the party. As I write I can

1177: Undaunted

hear her yelling, "Shaq, what they do?" That's how she would greet me most of the time. Because we were both raised in Liberty City, we had a natural understanding of one another. We connected immediately—our relationship was synergistic. Although we both attended Drew, we didn't become friends until high school. That's probably reflective of the solitude I experienced and created during that time in my life, I felt like an outsider—I felt awkward. I was nothing but skin and bones and I never had the latest clothes. And because our water was off at times, I would come to school smelling like a bag of onions mixed with potted meat. I couldn't wash my coochie, ass, or armpits. Laughing to myself, I remember sitting in Mrs. Turner's eighth grade English class not wanting to be called to the chalkboard for fear of releasing the awful scent of funk that sat between my legs. When class was over, I'd sit and wait for everyone to leave. And when I finally got up, I'd press my arms against the side of my chest, clearly embarrassed about being musty. From time to time, I'd use the bathroom soap as a way to get rid of the stench. You know, the pink liquid soap with the metal spout at the end? In order to release the soap, you had to push up on the metal part. I'd take a hand full and wipe it underneath my arms, hoping to get some relief from the smell all of my classmates had become familiar with.

Robyne and I were always together, even outside of school. Because I was so embarrassed about the condition at my house, we hung out at hers. Chile, we had more roaches than a cheating man has excuses. And we also had rats, big ass rats. Upon entering the house, you could hear and see them scram once you turned the lights on. So no one was coming over, including Robyne. Our best times were when we'd skip school and hang out at the nearby park. Although Robyne's predicament wasn't as bad as mine, she had her own share of issues. She was being raised by a single mother and was the only girl in a house of three boys. So we found solace in getting away from the noise of our personal lives and engaging one another. Before hitting the park, we'd go to Winn-Dixie to get food. Lunchables were the item of choice. The turkey-and-cheese option was my favorite, and still is. For hours, we'd sit and talk about our parents, boys, and our future. Robyne would do most of the talking, though. She loved to talk and always took the longest time telling a story. She would give you every grainy detail of an event. Over the years, I learned to zone out when she became too talkative and perk up when she got to the meat of the story. That skill set was necessary in order to maintain a friendship with Robyne. I didn't mind, though. I loved her. Outside of my future boyfriend Robert, she was one of the only people my age who understood me. She accepted me and because of our relationship, I felt full—like I needed nothing else.

Chapter

Not What I Envisioned

Despite my deliberateness, I carelessly gave in to "Dub." Like most of the guys in the projects, Dub was a bad boy. He sold drugs and was also known for robbing people at gunpoint. But for some reason, he caught my eye. Dub was much older than me, a grown man, I believe. He stood about 5' 10" tall, had "De-Las," and a mouth full of gold teeth—a far cry from what I consider attractive now. I could hear Dub before I saw him. Coming from the back of the new projects, along the side of the railroad tracks, I could hear Dr. Dre and Snoop Dog rapping, "one-two-three and to the fo, Snoop Doggy Dog and Dr. Dre is at the do." *The Chronic* was undeniably the best hip-hop album of 1992 and Dub did an awesome job of advertising it. As I heard him approaching, I'd run to a window, following him with my eyes until he parked his emerald green Buick in one of our parking spaces. Unlike my first crush, Dub knew that I liked him and didn't think I was too good for him.

Aware of every one of his visits to the projects, I'd "coincidentally" make sure I was standing at our back door when he parked his car. This would give

1177: Undaunted

me some one-on-one time with him before he headed off to do God knows what. Dub eventually asked me out on a date; he wanted to take me to the movies. By now, Babalu was dating Larena. She also lived in the projects—on the row immediately behind ours. Larena was a drug addict so it was easy for Dub to persuade her to watch my siblings while he took me out. And before I knew it, the day I'd envisioned finally came. I was sitting in the passenger seat of Dub's car, on our first date. As you would expect, I was nervous. Not only was I sixteen years old, but I was also sitting next to a young man notorious for strong-armed robbery. I mean, anything could have happened to me. I could have been caught in the crossfire between him and someone he'd robbed. Hell, he could have robbed someone on the way to the movies. Nevertheless, I arrived to the theater untouched. And if my memory serves me correct, we went to a movie theater in Hialeah.

Going with the natural order of things, Dub paid for my ticket and bought me popcorn and soda. Not soon after the movie started, he was ready to go. Clearly understanding what this movie date was about, I told him that I wanted to see the movie in its entirety. And although I watched *Cliffhanger*, I cannot begin to tell you what that movie was about. My mind was extremely occupied by what was to come afterward. And outside of running out of the theater, hysterically, there was no way out. At that point I'd committed to what was to come.

We pulled up to the motel and Dub got out and went to the rental office. I surveyed my surroundings and noticed we were close to Bayside. The motel building was pink—dark pink. We parked close to our room, went upstairs, and immediately got into bed. After all of our clothes were off, he proceeded to put his dick into my coochie. Although I was being extremely stupid by getting into a car with a drug dealer and agreeing to have sex with him, I suddenly had a moment of lucidity. Before insertion, I asked him if he had a condom, and of course, he didn't. I mean, why would he? He knew that I was a virgin, which was why he was so anxious about being with me. And what did he care about getting me pregnant? His level of consciousness at that time in his life did not involve responsibility—to any degree. I told him that he had to get a condom, that I wouldn't do it without one. Grudgingly, he got up. Because he came back so fast, I assume that he either had one in his car or had gotten one from the rental office.

He put the condom on, inserted, pumped about four or five times and that was it. There was no kiss, caress, or rub. There was no concern. Well, not for me, at least. As most young girls do during this time in their life, I wondered what I was doing. All of the times I sat and fantasized about him ended in a couple-minute-long fuck. He went for a shower and I cried like a baby. I was beyond disappointed and ashamed of myself. This was likely the first time I'd let my desire for love from a man overshadow my common sense and self-respect as a woman.

When I finally got up, I looked down at the sheets and noticed they were stained with blood. Because I wasn't on my cycle, I knew the blood was a sign that I was no longer a virgin, signifying my transition into a world that would prove more than challenging for many years to come.

That same day I had dance practice at the Cultural Arts Center. ICCTDC's home was condemned so we were forced to practice in nearby schools and community centers. Our conversation upon arrival to the Cultural Arts Center was more than memorable. Dub shifted his gear to a parked position, looked over at me, and said, "You know you mine, right?" I was floored. What in the hell did he mean about me being his? Despite my constant thoughts about being his girlfriend, I no longer wanted to be associated with him, let alone a part of his life. Our motel experience killed everything. Emotion quickly left the building and common sense kindly took over. He had gold teeth, no legal means of supporting himself, and was uneducated. What did he think I was going to do with him? He wasn't going where I was going. Hell, he didn't know where I was going because we had never had a sensible conversation. I politely said "yes," got out of the car, and walked into the building where everyone was waiting to begin rehearsal. I never wanted to see Dub again.

Chapter 16

Babalu Without The Banana Boat

During our second year in the projects, Babalu was no longer the owner of the Banana Boat. Being children, we didn't ask questions, especially concerning adult matters. But I was always (and still am) interested in knowing what happened. I mean, the Banana Boat was like air to my dad. He cooked there, met most of his girlfriends there, and likely forged a lot of other meaningful relationships there. In addition, he was a musician who'd obviously committed himself to creating music and sharing it with the world. Later on, I heard a rumor: Leo, one of my dad's friends, had made a co-owner agreement with him, but later took over the business despite my dad's unwillingness to allow him sole ownership. From time to time, Babalu would perform at Leo's restaurant, but their relationship became strained, causing them to sever ties for good.

After the Banana Boat, Babalu took on work as an undercover taxi driver. He would transport Bahamians looking to take advantage of American product prices. Things were, and still are, so expensive in the Bahamas that Bahamians would

1177: Undaunted

carve out travel time each year in order to stock up on basic necessities: toothpaste, mouthwash, toothbrushes, underwear, soap, linen, etc. These visits could last a day or an entire weekend. I imagine that Babalu enjoyed this job. It afforded him time to socialize with fellow Bahamians—his favorite activity. Without even being present I can hear the conversations about the island, who they knew, where this building used to be, what corner such and such lived through—all in thick Bahamian accents.

Babalu would also provide the same services to his one and only aunt, Innie. Innie was my cousin Mae's mother. You know, the cousin I mentioned earlier who had struggled with drug abuse? Innie owned a straw market in Freeport, which required that she come to Miami in order to stock up on items she'd sold months prior. Babalu would always announce her arrival as if the queen were coming, which meant that we (the girls) would have to make sure the house was in tip-top shape. I'd be particularly excited about her visit because that meant I would be able to tag along.

Innie did most of her shopping in downtown Miami. I guess it was sort of a one-stop shop for her. She could get T-shirts, hats, and other knickknacks tourists would buy as gifts. She would also shop for her grandchildren, purchasing their required school uniforms and whatever leisure clothes their hearts desired. Although she never bought me any clothes, I was always grateful for the opportunity to go shopping with Innie. Not only did it allow me to be away from home, but I totally loved the sausage

Babalu Without The Banana Boat

sandwich she'd buy from the nearby stand. It was a welcome change, considering the mundane meals we had at home.

After a day of shopping, Innie would ask me to help her pack and itemize her purchases. I would have to take all of her receipts, document the quantity and cost of each item, and make sure she paid the least amount of money when she reached Bahamian customs. She had me doing all kinds of illegal shit. Before she left, she'd hand me five dollars for my services—a far cry from the amount of money she saved by having me fill out her customs forms.

Innie passed away from cancer in 2006. In retrospect, I believe her death hit Babalu hard. I came to understand that he was closer to her than he was his own mother, who was Innie's sister. I also came to understand that she supported him financially, especially when he lost the Banana Boat.

CHAPTER 17

DUKE

Duke's troubles began to manifest themselves way before we moved to the projects, and our transition there would make them even more glaring. Duke was Ya-Yow and Babalu's third child together. He had been named Konduko Tywan Buford, and someone found it necessary to shorten his name to Duke. When you look up his name you will find that it has royal meaning: a sovereign male ruler of a continental European Dutchy; a nobleman of the highest hereditary rank. I believe his life will eventually validate the meaning of his name.

Like most of my siblings, I don't remember a whole lot about Duke's early life. I guess that has to do with how close we are in age. My memories of Duke come alive during his preteen years. I imagine he had grown tired of our destitute state and took matters into his own hands. He started out stealing from us. Whenever you had a nickel or dime, you would have to hide it and hide it well because Duke would eventually find it. We'd be searching all over the house for our money—flipping pillows and mattresses—thinking we were going crazy because we had just seen it. Little did we know, our money was long gone. Duke had found it and spent it, probably hours before we discovered it was even missing. After exhausting all of our hiding places, we came to the conclusion that we would have to sleep with our valuables on our person. That was the only way we were sure that Duke wasn't going to find them. And even then, he'd managed to rip a couple of us off.

Eventually, Duke began to look outside of our house for things he wanted. I clearly remember the police bringing him home after he'd attempted to steal jewelry from the flea market that sat next to Zayre's on 54th Street and 12th Avenue. Prior to that, he'd been caught stealing from his teacher's purse at Orchard Villa Elementary. Duke had discovered her storage place, one of her desk drawers. Babalu came to the school and beat him in front of the class—this was back when that was allowed. But that didn't faze Duke. His will to steal repelled any degree of ass-whooping Babalu gave. And he could whoop some ass. In addition, there was no reinforcement at home. There was no guidance. Although Ya-Yow was there, she was absent, and Babalu spent all of his time at the Banana Boat. That only left me, his sister, who was only two years his senior. And what was I supposed to do with him?

I often wonder if Duke's foster home experience caused him to behave the way he did. Duke was abused. His foster mother would lock him in the bathroom, alone, for hours at a time. She also made him take prescription drugs. As soon as this was revealed, Duke was removed and sent to live with one of our younger brothers, Chaz. They lived together

Duke

for the remainder of the year. I will never forget the time our foster parents brought us together for a visit. Prior to that, we hadn't seen each other in months. We all met at Duke and Chaz's house. When India and I pulled up, Duke was the first person I saw. His hair was cut into a mohawk and his face appeared dim. He looked sad. I immediately asked him who had cut his hair that way. His only response was a shoulder shrug that told me he didn't know.

Once we moved into the projects, that was it for Duke. He was surrounded by people who would endorse his criminal behavior and validate the nothingness he felt about himself. During this time, he was also introduced to drugs. When I first started my writing journey, I asked him to share his experiences. I wanted to include them in this book. I knew his story and perspectives were provocative, even more than mine. And what I read was beyond palpable:

Running out of money and time—this is when my troubled life started. My sister Charkes had to play the mother figure for the eight of us that stayed together. Now out of the trouble we had growing up, my dad moved to a place where at least 75 percent of the families never succeeded. Low-income rent, the projects were a sight to see. No one goes to school. Everybody's on drugs. It was lots of drug dealers and a lot of shooting. How could a man or female succeed? This was a different world to me. I never seen nothing like it before. I already had a problem with stealing and now I got a chance to get even better at it.

My dad enrolled me, India, and Simone into a

school about two minutes away from where we lived named Lilly C. Evans—an elementary school where nothing but project kids goes. I guess you know what that means. Yes, trouble. But I braced myself for it. My sister India was my classmate. Simone was in another class or two under me and India. A few weeks later came Chaz, Trea, and Eddie. They were very, very young. Charkes and Keo were at Charles R. Drew, one of the most popular middle schools in Miami. Charkes and Keo were headed in the right direction.

I never really liked school that much because it seemed boring to me. Plus, my dad had this thing where every time we ask him to buy us shoes or clothing, he would go get the cheapest shoes or clothing on the planet. That really made me not want to go to school. I was ashamed to walk into class with something nobody else had on or even seen. My dad was frugal. He would even go to the thrift shop to buy us clothing. Even when he was doing good financially, he still brought us "Bo-Bos." It didn't matter to him that I never wore a pair of Nikes or Reeboks growing up. It hurt me dearly to enter the class with a pair of XJ900s. So I decided, hey, I'm not going nowhere near school.

I never played hooky because of peer pressure. I never was a follower. I was in charge of a lot of organized criminal things. I was the one who made a lot of decisions. One day the school got broke into and whoever broke in took a lot of TVs. The next day I came to school they called me to the office and confronted me and I was like, "It couldn't have been me, I barely even come to school." So the principal said we are sending you to an opportunity school and I was shocked to hear and see that they accused me of doing such a thing. I *guess someone in the school labeled me as a criminal already at the age of twelve years old. At the time, it was 1991. Next thing I know I was going to Jan Mann Opportunity School, located in Carol City. I got up early in the mornings to get on the bus that had to come pick me up off of 22nd Avenue. I liked coming out early in the mornings at the time because I wanted to see what was really happening in that crazy world we lived in. Jan Mann wasn't so good itself. I started really skipping school even more because of some of the same problems I had at my previous school—financial ones. My dad even tried helping me for the first time in twelve years. He got me a job with one of his friends that had a car wash on 79th Street—Colley's Car Wash. My brother Keo was already working at the place before me. He was doing good for himself and had a little clout with the owner, which made me somewhat okay with working there. But after a while that played out for me too. Around that time someone introduced me to marijuana so I smoked every piece of money I made.*

By 1992, I was in full swing on the streets. Where we lived at was drug infested, full of drug dealers. I had gotten very familiar with a lot of them. All of them liked me because of my attitude. Somehow I had turned into a professional thief. I would go out to the USA Flea Market every time they opened the door and get whatever I wanted. I first started out stealing jewelry. The flea market was full of Arab and Japanese people who owned jewelry booths. I saw them as crooks themselves because of the prices they sold their jewelry for. I was the best ever to do the things I did in the flea market. It was people buying gold at the booth that I decided to steal from. I didn't care if anyone saw me just as long as they kept quiet. I would end up stealing a couple of thousand dollars' worth of jewelry. I would walk right up to the booth and make sure that the salesman were very busy and I would reach my hand over the counter and slide the glass back that secured the jewelry and take at least a whole tray of gold with no problem. I was very brave with it too. Then I would put the tray underneath my shirt and walk right out of the place with no fear. Then go to the projects and sell everything for cheap. I had rings that had all sorts of prices on them. The lowest was twelve hundred dollars and the highest was twenty-five hundred dollars.

I was very young at the time and had no one with me to really help me be a good salesman so I became the worst salesperson on the planet. I would sell a ring for one hundred dollars and the dudes that was buying the merchandise from me loved the hell out of me because a lot of them was getting over on me. I made stealing jewelry one of my financial resources. It became an everyday thing for me. It was also easy for me.

I was introduced to cocaine by a girl well known to my family. She also lived in the projects. She came over my house one day and asked me where my dad was. I told her he was not at home and she asked if she could use my bathroom. After I told her yes, she came in, ran upstairs, and about a minute later she asked me to come upstairs. I walked upstairs to see what she wanted. Then she asked me if I wanted to smoke a joint. She walked into the girls' room and pulled out some weed and a blunt and asked if I knew how to roll. I said, "Yeah." She then gave me the weed and the blunt and soon as I started to roll the joint she pulled out something that I quickly discovered as cocaine. She took a few bumps and asked me if I wanted some. I hesitated at first but then said, "Sure, let me get some." I took about two bumps myself and gave it back to her. Then she asked me to put some in the weed. I grabbed it and started dumping it in the weed. I handed it back to her. She was a real junkie at the time too. She took a few more bumps and then pulled out some cigarettes and started undoing the tobacco in one of them. Then she stuck the head of the cigarettes in the plastic baggy of cocaine and made what we call a raw square. She lit the cigarette, then told me to light the joint. We smoked both at the same time. I never been to space before but after smoking that stuff, I was on Mars. I was high as a kite. She had to go somewhere after it was over and I had to go somewhere too. I can't tell you where she took off to but I can tell you that I wasn't trying to come back to earth. I had to find a way to stay just like I was, away from all my pain. The next day I felt bad. I thought to myself—this is not how I went to sleep. I went to the flea market saying to myself, I'm not leaving until I clean the place out. Not having a clue of what the day might bring, I didn't even care at all. I knew that something had to give. I needed money to get back to where I was the night before. I came up that day and had a lot of bracelets. I went in and did my normal thing. I had no problem that time either. I sold a lot of the bracelets, dirt cheap again, only because I was trying to get some money right away for more drugs. I got enough money just to get what my soul was so badly calling for.

I went to the front row to where we lived at to buy some weed and cocaine. I never had to go far for drugs because they were right outside my front door. We were close to one of the biggest drug holes in the projects, "Scutter Hole." And it was all run by women. The boss lady, Sandy, was my friend. She was a slender, red chick that stood about 5'7" and weighed about 105 pounds. Despite her size, she was bigger than the streets. Most dope was brought from her. It got so bad that I was going to steal every day to get dope.

I eventually hooked up with a dude named Mike that lived on the same row as we did. He wanted to be down with me. At the time he didn't know I had already made a reputation for myself with the stealing. By then, my nickname was "Gold Hands." Mike became my sidekick. I gave him a job looking out and body-guarding. He was over 6' tall, making him perfect protection. But after a few trips in and out of the flea market, it came to an end. We had been noticed by someone. So every time we would go to get some jewelry, the salespeople would say, "Hey, stay away from my booth, both of you." But I know what went wrong: the tall dude (Mike) and the short dude (me). You get it? There were too many people involved and I made a mistake in letting Mike go with me. I eventually changed my game up.

I then started targeting purses. If a lady was walking around in the flea market, she had better have an alarm on her purse. If not, she will be crying before she left the place. I even seen a few with their purse wide open on their shoulder. I went from stealing gold to pickpocketing women's purses. Although I only did this a few times, the payoff was good. I was able to get one lady for a bank envelope with twelve hundred dollars in it. I walked up right next to her as she was standing at a jewelry booth looking at something she wanted to buy. I moved in close to her to where it looked like I was interested in buying something myself. She didn't even acknowledge me standing by her. I didn't have one dollar to buy anything. So when I saw that white envelope in her purse, I knew I had hit the jackpot.

I moved in really close and stuck my hand right in her purse, using two fingers to grab the white envelope that was sitting straight up in her purse without her feeling a thing. And because I was a professional, her purse didn't even move. I walked out of the flea market, put the envelope in my pocket, and jumped on the orange-and-white jitney that took me home. I went crazy that night. I must have messed up about eleven hundred dollars on cocaine.

After a few more purse events, I got bored again, causing me to steal beepers and cell phones off of women's purses. Then, I got Mike back on my team and we started stealing clothes, electronics, and whatever else we could get our hands on. But then, a lot of bad things started happening. The entire flea market started noticing us because of our daily tours. I eventually laid off for a minute. Mike went to selling drugs and watching out for "Creeper." That was easy for him because Creeper's headman was Sam, his sister's boyfriend. In addition, Mike's sister would play the "hold down girl" for Sam. That means that she would keep the drugs in her house.

Although Creeper was the shit at the time, I had no patience for the drug game. It was too slow and took a different type of hustle to make money. The competition was crazy too. You know Creeper wasn't the only drug hole in our neighborhood, right? I later on started a new way of getting paid. One night, me, Ricky, and Sleet went walking at about two in the morning. We spotted a guy walking up the north side of 7th Avenue. Although all of us spotted him at the same time, I was the only one excited about doing what we were about to do. I had a chrome .25 automatic handgun that had a pearl pink handle. So getting him was a sure thing. We started at him as fast as we could. And as soon as we approached him, I pulled out my gun and told him to give me everything he had. He was stunned. His mouth dropped open and remained that way. I guess he couldn't believe he was staring down the barrel of a gun held by a twelve-year-old. We all searched him. I went in his back pocket and pulled out his wallet. I opened it and found nothing, not even five dollars. He then looked down at me and asked that I give his wallet back. He must have had all of his important stuff in there—like his driver's license, Social Security card, etc. Sleet then directed us to go. And just as we started walking away from the guy, we discovered a police car cruising down 7th Avenue. Anxiously, I turned around and noticed that the guy we'd just attempted to rob spotted the police too. He flagged him down and when we saw the police stop for the guy, we took off running. We ended up at the Checkers that was around the corner from where we had just tried to rob the dude. The police cornered us and shined their bright lights in our faces. The light was so bright it lit up the whole building. Immediately, I dropped the gun. I was able to do so before the police got close enough to see it in my hand. And because we were standing in ankle-high grass, the police never saw the gun.

Apparently, the guy told the police what we'd just done. He got out of the car and immediately directed us to get on the car's hood, facedown, while he opened the back door so that we could get in. And thirty minutes

Duke

later, we arrived at the juvenile detention center. Ricky and Sleet were released. But I had to stay. By then, I'd made a name for myself, and the detention center's staff knew exactly who I was. I'd been arrested and sent there for petty theft, snatching a purse (after which I got caught on the scene by a hero), and burglary. So there was no way they were going to let me go. In addition, they knew Babalu didn't want me. He had already washed his hands of me. He'd gone to court and told the judge that he couldn't control me. That eventually turned me into an animal. I was hurt to hear my dad say that he didn't want me. Luckily, I had an awesome judge. He dropped the charges with the expectation that I go live in a group home. I was overjoyed—not because of the group home, but because I knew it wouldn't be long before I was going back to where I belonged—back to the projects.

As time went on, things got worse for Duke. He'd developed a wreckless reputation and Babalu had grown less sympathetic to and more intolerant of him. Despite Babalu always telling officers to take Duke to jail, they always brought him home first. Unlike now, police officers were sensitive to what was going on in the inner city and wanted to help. Once, Duke had gotten caught stealing from a store's register at the USA Flea Market. He was accompanied home by two police officers. They invited themselves in, walked into the living room, and had Duke sit on the couch as they talked to Babalu. I sat next to Duke. I was afraid for him. I knew he would be taken to the juvenile detention center again. And despite his dysfunction, I didn't want that for him. I was a worried parent. Suddenly, Babalu interrupted his conversation with the officers and said, "Y'all betta catch him, cause he gon run." And before Babalu could finish his sentence, Duke had darted out of the door and ran through the P.E. drug hole. Oh, did I forget to tell you that he was fast as hell? The police never caught him.

Eventually, Babalu forbid Duke entry into the house. He would tell us, especially me, not to open the door for him. Duke spent his nights on the street, stealing, robbing, and selling drugs. He would grow tired just before sunrise, at which point he'd look for somewhere to lay his head. Because everyone else would be fast asleep and I would be the only one up that time of morning getting ready for school, I was the perfect target. In addition, Duke knew that I had a soft spot for him. My sensitivity to him as my brother and my child caused me to give in, despite what Babalu had directed me to do. I can see him now, climbing up the wall to our tiny bathroom window (where I always stood doing my hair) and begging me to open the door so that he could go to sleep. "Please, Charkes," he would say. And within seconds I would creep downstairs and quietly let him in. I would always tell him not to reveal that I had opened the door. I never knew what happened once Babalu had discovered him, and by the time I'd gotten home from school, Duke would be on the streets again.

By the time I was ready to leave home for college, Duke had completed numerous sentences in the juvenile detention center. He had also been the ward of numerous "second-chance" programs.

Nothing affected him, though. He was eventually labeled as a "habitual criminal." Duke was only in his early teens.

In 1999, after our mother was laid to rest, Duke was arrested for felony gun possession and strong-armed robbery, giving him two life sentences in prison. Fortunately, on July 1, 1999, Florida had passed and implemented one of the country's most stringent gun laws, 10-20-Life (Florida Statue 775.087). Also known as "Use a Gun and You're Done," the 10-20-Life law is a mandatory minimum sentencing law in the state of Florida that primarily regards the use of a firearm during the commission of a forcible felony. With the intention of mitigating the use of weapons in Florida, Jeb Bush proposed this law as a reaction to the high number of instances when guns were being used in violent crimes in the state. The law enforces three mandatory sentences:

1. Producing a firearm during the commission of certain felonies mandates at least a ten-year prison sentence.

2. Firing a gun mandates at least a twenty-year prison sentence.

3. Shooting someone mandates a minimum sentence of twenty-five years to life regardless of whether a victim is killed or simply injured.

In 2000, the state legislature extended the mandatory sentences to cover sixteen- and seventeen-year-olds who fire a gun during a violent crime, as well as offenders with prior criminal records.

To date, Duke remains incarcerated. After filing multiple appeals, finally one was heard. For the last three years he has been sitting in the Miami-Dade County jail awaiting an appeal decision.

CHAPTER

DOING ME

As life does, it went on and I began to take a little more control over my life. I got tired of Babalu and his shenanigans so I became rebellious. I'd talk back and would always remind him of how much I disliked my life at home. His response was always the same: "When you leave this house, you will probably be worse off." That didn't matter because, in my mind, there was nothing worse than being his daughter. A couple of times, I ran away. I didn't go far, though—just to my girlfriend's house. I'd lie to her mom, telling her that my dad was okay with me spending the night. Funny thing was that when I got home, Babalu never said a word. I guess he understood what I was going through. Not punishing me conveyed a sense of empathy—a rarity for him.

By my eleventh grade year, I'd gotten a boyfriend. He was from Liberty City and lived across the street from the Pork-N-Beans projects, not too far from Miami Northwestern Senior High. Although we had gone to Drew together, we officially met at the Sun-

1177: Undaunted

Street Festival, an annual parade event that highlighted Miami-Dade County's accomplishments, culture, and businesses. The parade portion of the festival usually traveled north on 7th Avenue. My siblings and I were always there because Babalu usually sold food and we were required to help. He would set up shop right in front of the Banana Boat, selling conch salad, scorched conch, and conch fritters. And after the parade was over, we were usually allowed to enjoy the remaining festivities. That year, 1992, I'd gone over to the nearby meat market where the jam was taking place. A jam is an event where a DJ plays music outdoors in an open area. This could be on a corner, in a community, in a parking lot, or during a special outdoor event. Those in close proximity would hear the music blasting from the wall of speakers and immediately congregate and dance until their hearts were content. And that day, I was a part of the congregation.

The music was palpable. I could feel every vibration of the bass, and the treble was so loud it made my ears ring. I didn't care, though. I was out among the crowd and enjoying the music. And then I heard:

"Doom . . . Shai . . . Doom-Doom-Doom . . . coming right back atcha baby . . . oooh-ooh-oooooh-ooooooooh . . . if I ever fall in love again . . . the next time the lady will be just-like-you . . . Oooh-oooh-ooooh-oooooh. The very first time that I saw your brown eyes, your lips said hello, and I said hi, I knew right then you were the oooooone. But I was caught-up-uh in phy-si-cal attraction, much to myyy satisfac-tion; baby, you are more than just a frieeend. And if I eh-ever fall in love

Doing Me

again, I will be sure that the lady is a friend. And if I eh-ever fall in love so true, I will be sure that the lady's just like yoooouuuu—Ohhhhhhhh."

It was the one of the hottest R&B songs of 1992. Everyone was in a trance, probably thinking about a significant other or someone they had hopes for in that capacity. Before the second verse was complete, I turned to my left and there he was. We caught each other's eyes but I quickly looked away, playing coy. Eventually, he walked over to where I was—at the front of the crowd. We conversed a little and exchanged numbers. And from that point on, we were an item.

Robert was tall and lanky, and he had an extremely handsome face. He was the eldest of his mother's two boys. And although they were only two years apart, Robert was a father figure to him. Their dad had passed away when they were little and their mother was present but absent, like Ya-Yow had been. Robert protected his brother just like I did with my siblings. He made sure his brother went to school and he was always present at his extracurricular activities. I guess you could understand why we liked each other. Robert and I would hang out often. We spent the majority of our time standing on the sidewalk in front of the new projects and talking. For hours we'd talk about school, work, and both of our home lives. During those conversations, I also made sure he stayed in school so that he could graduate. Not having adequate guidance at home was difficult for young men like Robert. And at any moment, he could have decided that he was going to forsake his education for the streets.

1177: Undaunted

Although I'd already had sex, I made Robert wait. My first experience forced me to. I'd learned that I needed to build some sort of foundation before letting a man connect with me in such a way. (As an adult, I continue to struggle with that.) Now, I'm not going to sit here and say I was an angel. I gave Robert "blue balls" on a regular basis. We would go over to his nonbiological aunt's house—who happened to be the biological aunt of one of my closest friends at the time—and bone until he couldn't take it anymore. My coochie would be extremely wet and his dick would be rock hard but he never pressured me into having sex. It wasn't a condition of our relationship.

It was time for prom. Because we went to different schools, a decision had to be made about whose prom we would attend. We definitely couldn't afford to go to both. It wasn't a hard decision to make, though. Neither one of us thought there was anything exciting about going to Braddock's prom so we opted to attend Miami Northwestern's. The theme was "A Nubian Night on the Nile." I wanted our outfits to be in concert with the theme, so African attire it was. I was working for Ms. Nichols, teaching the babies, so I had my own money. I didn't have to worry about the disaster that occurred when I ran for queen of my middle school. It was a calamity of a pageant because I didn't have the money to purchase an actual gown. So I settled for an all white, lace number that made me look like I was a member of the youth usher board.

Doing Me

Wanting the perfect dress, I decided that I would have mine made. I searched high and low for material that was elegant while maintaining the spirit of Africa. I eventually found a beautiful gold-based material and purchased enough to make my dress and Robert's bowtie and cummerbund. My hip-hop teacher's mom was a seamstress so I hired her to make my dress. I told her that I wanted something off the shoulder and fitted but not too tight. The finished product was more than I imagined. It was beautiful. The neckline was sweetheart-shaped and the hem fell just above my ankle. I also had a shawl that was lined with a soft, black netted fabric. A stylist in the flea market did my hair. She had managed to put my hair up in a beehive using thick braids. You couldn't tell me anything. Not only was I cute, but I also made it all happen on my own. The finishing touch was my nails. I believe they were either natural or a light gold color. But as things go, I ended up breaking one while taking a bath. I must have run my hand across something that caused the top half of my fourth nail to break. So when you look at my prom picture, you will notice that my visible hand is only showing two fingers. I looked like I was throwing up a peace sign.

Our prom was perfect, though. Robert picked me up in a car he had rented and the remainder of the night was filled with dancing, goofing around, and keeping Robert's hands off of my ass. He wanted me in a bad way, and how could I blame him? I had him waiting damn near a year. Needless to say, my second experience was a different one. Robert held me, caressed me, and kissed me. He made love to me.

CHAPTER

MOVING ON

Despite all of the skipping Robyne and I had done, we managed to graduate from high school. I'm not sure about my buddy but my graduating GPA was a mere 1.9. This proved to be problematic with college acceptances. Still, I applied to Bethune-Cookman College in Daytona Beach, Florida, and Florida State University in Tallahassee. Both accepted me, but Florida State offered an acceptance under the condition that I report to school a month in advance to attend remedial courses. And believe it or not, I was offended. I, by no means, was a dummy and I was not going to be treated like one. They'd realize that if they knew how I'd forged my dad's signature on all of my college and loan applications. Needless to say, I accepted Bethune-Cookman's offer and used the remainder of my summer preparing for my transition.

Proudly, I handed Babalu a ticket to my graduation He quickly glanced it and asked, "What
n." He
Larena.
ded the
a ticket

for her, he wasn't going. Larena and I weren't the best of friends so I'd rather die before giving her a ticket to anything, including my graduation. During the two-plus years she and Babalu were together, we had had countless arguments. Her presence made me feel like I wasn't needed. She cooked, cleaned, and took up the space in my dad's life that I'd held since Ya-Yow left. The thing I hated most was when she would tell my siblings what to do. I used to say, "Who in the hell does she think she is?" That was my job and my job only. I remember an instance when my brother Trea needed money for a field trip. He'd asked Babalu, and like he always did, Babalu told him no. Trea stood in the kitchen, near the back door, sobbing. The next thing I heard was Larena telling him to shut up. Immediately, I intervened. I told her not to talk to him in that way and to leave him alone. She yelled to my dad, "Edison, you betta come and get this damn girl before I slap her." My facial expression and mouth replied, "Who are you going to slap? Not me." Babalu heard us arguing and intervened. He yelled at me, telling me that I needed to respect his woman. Crying hysterically, I told him how he needed to respect me because I had been taking care of him and his kids for the past decade. As soon as I got my last word out, Babalu slapped me across the face. I couldn't believe it. Before then, Babalu had never laid a hand on me. I stood in the very spot where he'd slapped me, holding my face, feeling betrayed. How could he have done such a thing? As fast as I could, I walked to the kitchen and called my sister Sherrae. She was one of Babalu's eldest daughters from a previous marriage and the one of the only adults who understood me. She was always outspoken about the way Babalu treated me and his need to let me be a little girl. Within the hour, Sherrae was at our house. I had already told her what happened, so when she got there Babalu was the first person she wanted to see. By this time everyone was standing outside, looking concerned and fearing what was to come. And after about ten minutes of talking to Babalu, I was in the back of Sherrae's car, heading to her place. I wouldn't return home for several months.

Graduation day came, and I was super excited. We all marched into Florida International University's gymnasium with our heads high, feeling proud of our accomplishment. I kept looking out into the crowd and at the door to see who'd come to support me. Eventually, I spotted Sherrae and her husband, Kevin. They were sitting to my right. Then, it was time for my row to approach the stage. Even during my walk, I continued to look for him. I walked up the steps and then onto the stage. Principal Bertani extended his left hand, offering my degree. I proudly grabbed it and thanked him with my right hand. On the way to my seat, I looked over the audience again to see if he changed his mind but he was nowhere to be found. Turned out Babalu stood by his word. He didn't attend my high school graduation.

After a long summer, it was time for me to go. I had spent three months preparing for that day, but I was far from ready. From our bathroom window, I could see Sherrae and Kevin approaching our house.

1177: Undaunted

They'd rented an SUV because I needed the space for my luggage. Once they parked, I walked downstairs to meet them. My bags were packed and by the door. Babalu wasn't there and I was neither surprised nor hurt. After all, he didn't even attend my graduation. My siblings were at home, though—waiting just like I was. As Kevin packed my things away, I could see the looks on their faces. They were sad and in disbelief. They knew that I would be going away to school but likely never believed it—well, at least their hearts didn't. As soon as Kevin was done, I quickly got into the car. Actually saying good-bye was too painful. I imagine they were wondering what they would do without me. Who would cook for them? Who would wash their clothes? Who would look after them? We eventually pulled away. And while I was getting ready to embark on one of the most important journeys of my life, my thoughts were with the most important people in my life—my brothers and sisters. But I had to move on.

Appendix

Babalu in his early "20s"

Babalu when he was a fire dancer,
before "Babalu and His Head Hunters"

Ya-Yow in her early "20s"

Front, left to right: Trea, Chaz, Little Eddie
Back, left to right: Simone, Keo, India, Duke

Ya-Yow with (front to back):
Little Eddie, India, Chaz, Trea, Simone

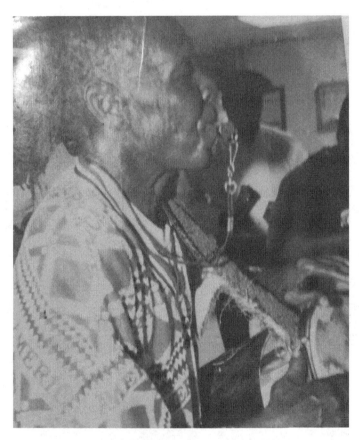

Babalu playing Junkanoo at a party

Left to Right:
Me, India and Simone dancing at a church event

Left to right: India, Simone, Ms. Nichols, Me
at Simone's Dance Recital, 2015

Me (far right) at Orchard Villa Elementary.
This is a photo of the "Say No To Drugs" group

"1456 N.W. 60th Street"
Our landing spot after leaving the foster home

When we lived between 15th and 17th avenue,
on 69th street

Old home of "Inner City Children's Touring Dance Company" (ICCTDC)

Robert and I, 2013

Sherrae and I, 2015

Simone's wedding day, 2011

Me, 8th grade prom, 1988

Shadeaw and I, 2016

Me standing on the corner of 21st ave. and 7th Street, The "Scotts"

Christmas 2008. Front to back:India, Todd (my friend), my son, Adrian, Babalu and Simone

Little Eddie, Chaz, and Trea. Thanksgiving, 2014

Me at work. Jackson Memorial Hospital, 2014

Made in the USA
Lexington, KY
03 April 2016